YOU ARE THAT!

VOLUME II

Sri Ramana Maharshi

Sri H.W.L. Poonjaji

(*Papaji*)

YOU ARE THAT!

VOLUME II

SATSANG WITH GANGAJI

YOU ARE THAT!
VOLUME II

Front cover photo: Eli Jaxon-Bear
Cover Design: Jennifer Miles

Third Printing. Printed in the USA on acid-free, recycled paper.

ISBN # 1-887984-00-3
Library of Congress Catalog Card # 95-71521

CONTENTS

Formal satsangs are public gatherings, open to everyone, in which Gangaji interacts with those asking questions, giving reports, or making comments.

You Are That! Volume II contains selected excerpts from satsangs held throughout 1993-1995 at various locations in Northern India, Nepal, Bali, and the Western United States, including Maui, Hawaii.

Throughout these pages, words such as That, the Beloved, It, Self, and Truth are in reference to that vast, unnamable, eternal Presence; sometimes called God, Christ-Consciousness, Buddha-Mind, existence, awareness, or whatever term used in the vernacular of each particular culture and sub-culture.

The Search for Enlightenment

You have imagined yourself to be a body, and in this imagination, you are frantically trying to find the secret to the liberation of that body. Maybe you have studied certain Eastern spiritual traditions, or maybe you have studied certain Western spiritual traditions. Maybe you have been involved in certain acquisition activities. All of these *doing-to-get* activities are related to the liberation of your body.

Your body cannot be liberated. Your body is doomed to disappearance. Your body is bound by birth, hunger, disease, death, genetics, and environment. However, if you turn your face to That which permeates your body, That which surrounds your body, That which your body arises in, exists because of, and returns to, you meet freedom itself. This meeting is liberation.

The concept of enlightenment comes from the recognition or the insight, *My God, I have been living in ignorance. I want to leave ignorance.* This recognition is an evolutionary point in a life-stream.

People first come to the spiritual search from an egocentric idea of what will be attained. The beginning of the spiritual search is the positive aspect of ego, "I'm tired of suffering. I want to be happy. I hear happiness is the spiritual goal." *I want to be happy* is a thought that comes from a developed ego, a functioning, integrated ego.

With courage and guidance, there arises the resolve to turn away from the forces that support ignorance, and to turn toward the forces that support enlightenment. All of this is immeasurably important.

The search for enlightenment takes innumerable forms. Perhaps first is the attempt to follow the code and practices of religion. Usually next is the attempt to throw off the code of religion and live by a personal code. There may be superficial hope that in dressing or acting as the Buddhists or Hindus or Sufis dress and act, some of their accumulated attainment will transfer. However you have tried to get enlightenment, you have continually come to what appears to be a dead end. At this end, rather than experiencing *end*, the search usually begins with a new or different code or religion or rebellion.

You cannot find true happiness by *doing* anything. You can experience moments of happiness, certainly. But to recognize you are that which *is* happiness, you must abandon all vehicles of escape. The end must be experienced. I am speaking of giving up every *thing*.

What a surprise to realize that real happiness requires releasing everything! To receive ultimate attainment, finally you must stop trying to *get* anything. The idea of *you* must end. When you give up the idea of enlightenment, you realize what the idea of enlightenment points to.

If you can see that what you *thought* you wanted has not given you what it is you *really* want, then you are ready. You are mature. Maturity has little to do with age or education or spiritual practice. Maturity reflects ruthless intelligence in telling the truth. The truth is that no matter how much you have enjoyed your relations and circumstances, those things have not given you that which is lasting and eternal.

This recognition is a rude awakening, a disillusionment. Until disillusionment occurs, there is a trance-like state where you wander through life attempting to grasp the things you want and reject the things you don't want in the hope of receiving lasting happiness.

Through disillusionment, rude awakening, and ruthless truth telling, you can actually discover what you really want. If by luck what you really want is eternal truth, then have the courage to stop looking in any *thing* for eternal truth. Whether your search is in worldly things, philosophical things, or spiritual things, just stop looking. When you stop looking, you can discover eternal truth. It takes less than an instant.

You are very lucky if you have the desire for truth, but in your search for truth, what is searched for is an image or an idea or some concept based on what you have been taught, or what you have read, or what you imagine to be so, or what you remember from some glimpse in the past. These are all mental *things*. They may be beautiful things, but even the most subtle mental concepts are still things.

The great gift offered by my Master, Sri Poonjaji, and by his Master, Sri Ramana Maharshi, is the instruction to *Be Still*. To not look to the mind as the reference point of who you are.

What can be said about what is revealed in stillness? Much has been said that points to it. Nothing has been said that can touch true revelation. Words such as infinity, eternity, grace, Self, Truth, God, all point to that which is revealed in absolute stillness. Yet the moment that which is revealed is conceived as some *thing*, then revelation also points away from truth.

That which you are is untouched by any idea of ignorance or enlightenment. While the concept of enlightenment points to freedom and the truth of one's being, if you cling to the concept, you overlook what was present before you ever heard the word. You overlook what is present when your body is in the deepest sleep state. You overlook what remains when your body is long gone.

There comes an instant when by some miraculous, mysterious grace, you are struck dumb of all words, all concepts, all searching, all striving, all identification. In that moment, an instant out of time, there is the realization that who you are, really are, has never been touched by any concept. This very instant of realization is, in fact, what the concept of enlightenment points to.

The habits and tricks of mind, of course, are very strong, and they may reappear. You may think, *Oh, I got it! I'm enlightened now.* This thought is already a trick of mind. This thought already presupposes some entity separate from consciousness, separate from that which is revealed in the instant of the ceasing of mind activity. In thinking, *Oh, I got it. I'm enlightened,* there must also follow, *Oh, I lost it. I'm unenlightened.* You must have been through this many times. Both concepts are opposite sides of the same coin. There is suffering in both. They both come from the thought, *I am some thing, and enlightenment is some other thing I must get to be happy.*

Who you are has no need of, no desire for, and no fear of either ignorance or enlightenment. Who you are is free of any concept. The concept of enlightenment points to realizing that. The concept of ignorance points to not realizing that. The moment you cling to any concept of ignorance or any concept of enlightenment as reality, you are already in the experience of ignorance again. Do you see how subtle the workings of the mind are?

Mind includes all thought, whether mental, physical, emotional, or circumstantial. All trickery of mind is based on the idea that you are some *thing.* You are no *thing* at all. Everything that appears, appears in the vastness of eternal truth. When you identify yourself as a *thing*—mental, physical, emotional, or circumstantial—and you believe this identification to be real, you overlook the reality of the vastness of Being.

Realization is so utterly simple, and this simplicity is what has held it as the deepest secret, inherently protected by the corrupting power of the mind. All striving, all practicing, all comparing, and all codes are realized as irrelevant in the vastness of this utter simplicity. In the moment of realization, there is ultimate freedom, eternal truth. The radiance of truth melts the mind into blissful submission to the unnamable. If there is the slightest clinging to any *thing,* then once again, the mind is caught in misidentification, and suffering is experienced.

The opportunity for your particular mind-stream is to realize that you are the animating force which gives the mind-stream its apparent power. This gift from Ramana, through Papaji, is the invitation to stop midstream, to stop and recognize who you are. This can be realized immediately in simply being still. You will never realize it by searching for it in thoughts. You may have intellectual understanding, but you will never be fully satisfied until you embrace your Self—the truth of who you are.

You cannot *make* stillness. You *are* stillness. Be who you are. Be still—absolutely, completely still—and see that which is before any thought, any concept, any image of who or what or when or how or why.

Stillness is presence of Being. You are that presence of Being. Receive your Self. Drink your Self. Be nourished by your Self. Begin your exploration of That.

I do not mean explore your thoughts. You have explored your thoughts, and they have taken you as far as they can take you. I do not mean explore your emotions, your feelings, your sensations, or your circumstances. Explore your Self. That which is before, during, and after all objects of awareness. THAT. That presence of Being is who you are.

I am not attempting to teach you this. There is no way possible to teach who you are. There is no way possible to learn who you are. The message that I bring is simply that in the heart of awareness, you recognize without a shadow of a doubt the truth of your own being.

All that is required for that recognition is that you pull your attention back from the usual fixations and preoccupations. Let attention rest in the truth of satsang, formless and present as the core of Being.

The Challenge of Surrender

There may be strategic impulses to fight, to deny, to indulge, to pretend, to protect, to dismiss, and to trivialize; but deeper than all those is the call to just be. In surrender to being, an even deeper surrender is revealed. Be. Be more. Discover if you can find a limit to being. For this discovery, you must surrender all ideas of who you are, where you are, how you are, what you are, when you are, and more. Surrender all ideas to pure beingness and then see.

The more you surrender, the more you are called to surrender. There is no landing strip where you say, "Now I am finished with surrender." You are called to surrender every possibility of landing—every concept of everything, every concept of nothing, every concept of yourself, every concept of other, and more.

Obviously, this is not a surrender in defeat. It is a victorious surrender. It is a surrender to peace. The peace that *is*. Surrender does not make peace or formulate peace, but reveals the peace that *is*.

Surrender all for one instant, and see what remains.

There may be great fear that something will be lost in surrender. But tell the truth, what have you ever been able to keep? Finally, of course, you cannot keep your body. You cannot keep all of your philosophies. All of your neat, tidy conclusions are finally gone, nothing, less than dust.

I am not inviting you to surrender to me, Gangaji. I am not saying surrender to your "higher" self. I am speaking of the surrender to Truth, to that which holds all.

The treasure in surrender uses everything as a signal for deeper surrender—good circumstances, bad circumstances, comfort, discomfort, beauty, and suffering. Fall deeper and deeper; no abiding anyplace, no landing anywhere.

• • •

You use the word surrender a lot.

It is my favorite word. Doesn't it strike terror in the mind? Oh, what sweet terror. Such sweet terror is this surrender.

Could you tell me what it means to surrender?

I can tell you what it doesn't mean to surrender. We can start there.

I do not mean surrender to your thoughts, which you have been surrendering to. I do not mean surrender to your emotions, which you also have been surrendering to. I do not mean surrender to particular circumstances. I mean surrender all thought, emotion, and circumstance to that which is bigger and deeper.

Surrender your identity. Surrender your suffering to that which is closer than identity, deeper than suffering.

Yes, I love the word surrender.

Do you discover victory or defeat in this surrender?

Are you asking me?

Yes! Let's not pretend to be satisfied with theory!

I don't know how to answer.

The only way you can answer is by surrendering everything for one split second. Just a split second of absolute, complete surrender, and then tell me, is this victory or defeat?

Let go of the theory. Right now, give up your name, give up your parents, your history, your relations, your possible future. Give it all up for one instant.

What is the result? What is the report from surrender?

It makes me think of—

Then give that up too.

(laughing)

You're getting closer. You're showing the signs now. Thoughts fall away; laughter starts.

Give it all up for one split second. You are quite free to pick it all up again. Just for a second, put all aside—very simply, very easily, very quickly. Tell me, in that split second, is anything wanted or needed?

It feels very spontaneous.

Yes, now even give up spontaneity. Give up any label of what it is. Give up any conclusion of what will be given you if you surrender. Do you understand? Many people try and make a deal: "I'll surrender *if.* I'll surrender if I get this, and this, and this." I am encouraging unconditional surrender.

You may think that to surrender means losing something. In reality, all that is lost is the power of your thoughts and emotions and circumstances to dictate a point of view about the reality of life. This is victory, the most sublime victory. It cannot be understood. It cannot be imagined. It can be directly experienced, and this is your opportunity. This is your time. This is the invitation of satsang.

How do I give it all up?

This is an essential question. Recognize how you have attempted to hold it all together. Then you will see that no attempt has ever been successful. Whatever the appearance of success, recognize it is finally impossible to hold it all together. Isn't that a relief?

There is a belief or mind-set or brain-washing which promises that you can hold it all together. This begins with the learning of your name. How many times did you have to hear your name before you learned to think, *Okay, yes, that is who I am.*

Your name is forgotten each night as you go to sleep and has to be remembered each morning. Of course, you get very used to remembering, so that when you come out of the sleep state, your name arises and you easily slip it on. Your occupation is waiting and you slip your occupation on. Success or failure is waiting. Worthlessness or superiority is waiting.

Now you can ask how to remain naked.

See that all you have put on is illusion, is make-believe. You are not your name, however well you have memorized it. You are not success or failure, however thoroughly you have evaluated circumstances. Recognize that it takes some degree of effort to recall and put on name, evaluation, conclusion, somebodyness. Simply see that you are, in fact, always truly naked. Recognize that illusion only appears to cover who you are. Realize the shining quality of presence that cannot be covered by your or anyone else's name and form.

Do you know the story of the Emperor's new clothes? The Emperor walks through the streets naked because he is deluded into thinking he has many different, very fine outfits. Because he is the Emperor, everyone wants to keep him satisfied and happy. Almost all his subjects say, "Oh, beautiful new outfit. Yes, that is very nice." Except for one young innocent who truthfully says, "But wait, you don't really have anything on. You are actually naked!"

This is the guru's purpose in your life. The guru says, "You think you are dressed poorly or dressed well, but your nakedness shines through in its glory, in its beauty."

Whatever you think you are clothed in is simply thought, and it is a weighty, unnecessary thought. Whether you clothe yourself with a thought of rightness or wrongness, who you are is naked beauty, glory, pristine no-thingness. Stop thinking otherwise and see. Then you don't have to go to the trouble of letting it all go. You will recognize, *Ha! There is nothing there anyway. What I thought I could hold on to is simply a thought, and thoughts are made of nothing. They seem to be something, and are experienced as something, but in reality, they are nothing.*

How to let it all go is a very good question. The only problem with the question is that it assumes there is something to let go of. This assumption is based on the naming process, the believing process, and the "acting as-if" process. Don't "act as if." Don't name. Don't process. Just be.

Sri Ramana Maharshi often said, "Be as you are."

To be as you are is to be before naming, before clothing. Be That. The effort is in the naming and clothing, and the following evaluation of what has been named and clothed, and the comparison of that with other names and clothes.

Be as you are. Then you will see as I see, and you will have a good laugh, a deep laugh, a serious laugh.

• • •

There is that truth which I know deeply, but to live it is a challenge for me.

Yes, the challenge of surrender is a great challenge. What a challenge! Don't you like a challenge? Of course you do.

Of course I do.

Yes! This challenge goes against the whole tide of conditioning. The challenge is the invitation to satsang. Satsang is not an escape from challenge, a hope that you can be defended against challenge. It is a penetration into the depth and the core of experience to see that which already exists, pure and unchallenged, with no need of defense, of protection, or even of maintenance. That which is your own Self.

When you are ready to meet this challenge, you are finished with whining about *why* and *them* and *me* and *should have* and *could have*. You are finished.

People sometimes have an infantile idea that a spiritual life is something like learning A, B, C, D; after which you get a good grade, a good evaluation, which proves you are very good. You graduate into the spiritual realm, and then you can go to sleep again.

A true spiritual life is the realization of the endless totality of Being as discovered in the heart of emptiness. Every moment of every day is a vehicle for that realization. Good times are beautiful, pleasant vehicles. Bad times are horrible, unpleasant vehicles. Still, all is revered as the vehicle for Self-realization.

This particular individuation experiences much frustration because it knows of boundlessness but identifies with the illusion so much of the time.

Just for a moment, acknowledge the sublime grace that allows you to say with all clarity and without pretense that you have experienced boundlessness. What a blessed life this is! What a graced life. Now give this grace more weight than you give the frustration.

If some previously suppressed or indulged tendency arises after this miraculous experience of boundlessness, how will it be met? In what context will it be viewed? The usual relationship with the arising of past tendencies is a scrambling of mental activity to either get something back or keep something away. In your case, frustration has arisen. Fine. Now frustration is the fire. Jump into the fire. Don't try to fix the frustration. Don't try to ignore it, overcome it, control it, or act it out. Directly experience frustration. Directly discover *who* is really frustrated.

I could be mistaken, but I feel like I've been sitting in this fire for a long time.

You are mistaken. To sit in this fire for even an instant reveals there is no entity suffering! There is only boundless freedom of being. So if you feel you have sat in it for a while, recognize that you are sitting in some idea of it, usually coupled with the idea of getting out of it. All of this presupposes some entity that is located someplace.

Ask yourself, "What if for every instant for the rest of the days of this particular experience of individuation there is only total, absolute frustration?"

Do you see what a relief this is? For an instant, if you stop fighting it, you see what exists in the core of frustration. Then you will directly discover the secret answer to *who* is frustrated.

Jump into the fire!

• • •

I have a fear of selling out, which I feel I've done many times, because normal life seems safer.

You have exposed your fear that you will turn your back again, that you will sell your soul again. Your willingness to expose that fear, rather than pretend the sell-out is not possible, is your resolve to be vigilant. Willingness exposes everything. The challenge of surrender is now even greater, because the temptation is to identify and attempt to cling to wherever there are good feelings.

I've tried that and it doesn't feel good at all.

Wonderful! This is wisdom speaking. It truly doesn't feel good to identify anywhere. Fall into surrender. Fall into truth. Fall into Self, endlessly. As long as there is the physical body in form, there is some sense of identification. As long as this sense is present, surrender it to sublime truth. Then the sense that you are the body is a gift. Then you are constantly surrendering to the unknown fire. A deeper surrender, a bigger surrender, with bigger stakes. This is life really lived; not through some kind of image of security, but directly, openly, not knowing.

It feels like a tremendous gift.

It *is* a tremendous gift. It is a gift beyond value. Honor the gift. Do not treat it casually. It is sacred. It is holy. Don't diminish it in any way and see. Let the holy gift live the life that you have called yours. Let the gift take over your life.

Blessedly, It takes what has always been Its. What was assumed to be yours is returned to its source.

The metaphor of Lucifer, God's very favorite angel, the angel of light, the angel of mind, is a story of, "My, me, mine. My power, my glory, my life, my actions, my attainments, my victories." Finally, blessedly, there is the return of mind to its source. Where does Lucifer get its power? When this is recognized, then Lucifer is no longer the devil, no longer in opposition, no longer in service to delusions of "me" and "mine." Then Lucifer once again can serve God. The mind can serve its source. The return is the surrender.

Let God have you. Give up every idea and every image of what God is. Stop placing a limitation on God. Let God have your life. It may not always be comfortable, but what is a life of comfort in comparison to this holy servitude?

Yes, don't sell your soul for comfort. It is a measly sell-out, and there is no rest in it. There may be a measure of momentary thrill or momentary cessation of pain, but you have done this too often. You know you will never be happy until you just surrender all your unnecessary burdens. Why postpone? Any postponement is more unnecessary burden.

• • •

I find myself donning the cloak of ignorance, rather than living by what I know to be so obviously true.

Yes, you have the choice to lie and hide in the labyrinth of the mind. When you choose not to hide, you choose to discover who you are.

You have chosen to hide from truth in assuming and believing and practicing that you are your name, body, history, emotions, and thoughts. The willingness to see is the willingness to give up the choice to lie, to hide, or to seek comfort in hope and belief. It is the willingness to experience the heart of annihilation. To see the outrageous truth that even in the attempts to hide, nothing is truly hidden.

You have freedom of choice. For a long time you have chosen to hide and then chosen to deny you are hiding. You have chosen to speak words of freedom and use concepts of freedom. Now you have the choice to be who you truly are. Realize who you are and you finally realize divine choicelessness!

In your imagination you have form, shape, characteristics, qualities, aspects, and these can be compared to other forms and shapes past, present, and future. There is nothing wrong with imagination. It just doesn't have anything to do with who you truly are. Imagination is an enormous power, and from that power come enormous experiences of pleasure and pain.

Finally, in a certain lifetime, there arises the desire to know who you *really* are. This is a very lucky lifetime. In that lifetime, satsang appears in your consciousness most unexpectedly. In satsang, you at least hear with your outer ears: "It is absolutely possible for you, at this time, in this moment, to discover the truth of who you are, and to live out the rest of the experience of this lifetime in devotional service to that."

You have always been that. In this particular lifetime you have the opportunity to discover what, in truth, you have always been. It is a very sacred moment. A serious moment, and a joyous moment. It is a moment of choice.

I congratulate you. Somehow you are drawn to discover what gives mind, body, imagination, illusion, and the whole cosmos its power. In this discovery, don't wait for anyone or anything. Don't wait, because it is right here, right now.

• • •

I had this thought, "Surrender to what?" But I guess it is just to simply surrender.

Surrender all of your suffering. Surrender all your ideas of *not now, shouldn't be, not me, can't be, too simple.* Just surrender them and see. As an experiment, surrender your doubt.

What about my resistance? How does it serve? What role does it play?

When you were a child, you played hide and seek, and at first you resisted being found. Then you began to recognize that actually you wanted to be found. There is a great joy in being found, even though you may have thought you had the perfect hiding place. Maybe now you begin to recognize that this game is actually about being found. You had thought it was only about hiding. The prelude is to hide, but the real pinnacle of this game you have played on yourself is to be found. Then you are done with resistance.

Resistance may arise, but let it arise in the willingness to be found. There may be the temptation to stay hidden, but still there is the recognition of something bigger in being found, regardless of expectations of how you will be found, when you will be found, or what it will look like when you are found. Opening your mind, opening your disguises, opening your resistance, is the announcement of availability to be found.

In speaking about resistance, already resistance is past tense. Don't give it a thought. Don't get in a relationship with it. When you sense a contraction, let it be. When you conclude that it shouldn't be, or that it should be different, then resistance is given more strength. Let it be, and it has no power.

You are welcomed to satsang in whatever state of mind. It doesn't matter. In just not obeying the urge to bolt, or the urge to close, or the urge to dismiss, there is the possibility that you will find your own Self.

Be found. Be eternally found. Finding is limitless revelation—so subtle, so immense, so indescribable. Find your Self everywhere.

So you could say, surrender to being found?

Yes! Yes!

• • •

My mind is quieter, but it wants to analyze and memorize. I tell myself to relax, be still, go deeper. I feel stuck, and then I start to feel separate from that which I am. Please help me to finally surrender.

Help is here. You are never separate from help. Anytime you ask for help, help presents itself. It is beautifully humbling to ask for help. It is good to give up your idea of independence. Just say, "Please help," and you will see instantly that every enlightened being of every realm known and unknown, from all the dimensions charted and uncharted, is immediately supporting, helping, reminding, pushing, pulling, embracing, holding, shaking—whatever is needed. Your plea for help cuts through all past arrogance. You are helped immediately because you are calling to the truth of yourself.

I know surrender is present now, but I also know that I'm very afraid of it. It's like I'm halfway to being fed, and then I open my mouth and say, "Don't feed me."

You opened your mouth, but then you closed your mind. You know the mind is closed if immediately you have an idea or image of what help should look like, when it will come, how long it will take, what it should do, and what it should not do. Isn't this the same old story? The replaying of this same old story is not truly asking for help. Help is not separate from the willingness to receive. The most profound help is already present just waiting to be called, just waiting to be invited, just waiting for you to finish this tedious game of hiding.

I haven't been able to just accept that the Self will have me.

You are wanted totally, completely, by your own Self. Freedom wants you as its own.

I am never speaking of freedom of the body or any image you have that you have named "me." The body is not free and doesn't need to be free. I am not speaking of emotional freedom. I am not speaking of the freedom to do what you want to do. I am speaking of freedom that is already free, silence that is already silent, happiness that is already happy. While you tell your story of unworthiness, already within you is an ocean of happiness. That is what's calling you. Open your mind to see.

• • •

You told me to relax completely, and now my doubt is that life will still be like it was before.

Then you are not relaxed. You are still chewing on doubt. It takes effort to follow the thought of doubt, and then the thoughts that follow those thoughts. Pretty soon you are obviously not relaxed.

To mentally relax, let go of all lines and ropes back into the past. Where is *before* in a still mind? To remember what it was like *before* requires some effort. See what it is like right now.

I am not saying you have to spend your life completely relaxed. You are free! You are free to struggle. You are free to be tense. You are free to follow all doubts. You are free to endlessly doubt. And you are free to just relax and be who you are.

Perhaps you have overlooked that you can relax. You can let your thoughts cease, and you can see what reveals itself.

You will see that you cannot be like you were before, because what you imagined you were like, you were not anyway! See what is right now, and see you have always been that.

• • •

I was going to tell you about how much I truly want realization, but upon radically honest inspection, I find that I cannot say anything except, "Help." I want to want reality, but find myself this morning face to face with my conditioning and the desires of lifetimes.

This is an important moment. You hear about enlightenment, or you hear about the possibility of realization, and you say, "Oh, yes. I want that. Great. That sounds wonderful . . . and then I'll be happy all the time. Then people will respect me. Then people will love me. Then people will give me what I want. Yes. I want that!"

That is all right. This is the way it first must be. There must be some appeal through the ego. But as you are drawn deeper into the truth of what keeps you unhappy, into what keeps propelling you through incarnation after incarnation of searching for happiness, there arises discriminating wisdom. It is at this point that true choice is possible.

When you are face to face with conditioning, the choice is real.

There is a kind of spiritual trance from which I hear people say, "I have no choice. It's all taken care of anyway. It's not my doing." This is conceptual garbage. You have absolute choice. You are consciousness itself. How can you not have choice? You have the choice to deny your Self, and you have the choice to affirm your Self. You have the choice to turn from your Self, and you have the choice to surrender to your Self. You have the choice to know who you are.

You have the choice to continue to say you have no choice. Just don't expect me to believe or accept it. It is a childlike idea of choicelessness. First make the choice. Then maybe you can say you have no choice and not before. Before that choice is made, the rest is just a theory of not having choice, a safety zone, a very flimsy excuse to suffer.

Now ask, "What do I really want?" When the pleasures of the senses arise, you can ask yourself deeper, "What will they give me? What is it I want from them?" If, in fact, what you are searching for is beauty, peace, love, and truth—good. You don't have to go anywhere for that. Face desires and temptations and they will burn in the facing. All is burned in that.

If what you want is more excitement, more stimulation, more imagery, more fantasy, then follow those desires, and report back to me what the result is.

• • •

How would you describe what would be the first step in controlling desires?

I appreciate the question, but instead of controlling desires, I suggest you surrender to that from which the desire arises. In order to discover where the desire arises, you have to turn right into the desire. The usual mental activity is either to be very afraid of our desires or very in love with them. The usual is to indulge desires, and through indulgence finally to discover that indulgence doesn't make for satisfaction. Indulgence makes for dissatisfaction. With indulgence, the demon of desire grows ever larger.

Some have also attempted to repress desires, and this repression usually leads to rigidity and covert indulgence.

Here I am speaking of simply meeting the very core of the desire itself.

Some desires will kill you if you meet them.

No. They may kill you if you indulge them.

That's not what you're speaking of?

I am not speaking of indulging. Do not move an iota either toward the desire or against the desire, but actually trace the desire back, with your consciousness, to where it arises.

You may have an overwhelming desire for alcohol or sex or some other activity that produces pleasure. So you have pursued alcohol or sex or whatever. You have pursued it, and you have pursued it, and you have realized the pursuit is killing you spiritually, emotionally, and physically. What I am speaking of is stopping the pursuit, stopping the rejection, and meeting the actual experience of desire.

Why don't you do it right now, and then see what the answer is. Then we are not speaking theoretically.

When you say to go towards it —

I believe you are misunderstanding *meet* as going toward, or feeding the desire, or giving it what you imagine it craves. I am not saying to *give* it anything. I am saying to stop all giving and stop all taking away so that you are naked in the power that is arising. In that nakedness, without moving the slightest to feed, to give, to reject, to ignore, or to control, discover directly what is at the core of the desire, what is at the root of it. In that, you discover directly what it is you are really desiring, having nothing to do with alcohol or sex or any other pleasure.

I can't figure it out.

The deepest teaching from Ramana directs us to *Be Still*. In being still, there may arise a momentum of past desires which previously have either been fed or rejected. Both feeding (indulging) and rejecting are egocentric activities and generate further karma, further suffering. In being still, you are finally naked in the direct experience of desire without moving the slightest to take care of that desire or the slightest to cover that desire.

I am speaking of a great burning, a great, intense fire. This fire burns away all that covers that which is permanently, eternally, desireless, in bliss. Be naked in the flaming consummation with one's Self as love and fulfillment.

Feeding desires can kill you. It has killed you over and over. Rejecting, ignoring, and controlling desires also has killed you over and over. Now you can face this death directly. You have learned from many millions of years of evolution about the feeding and rejecting of desires. This is known. Since it is known, you can now put it aside. What has not been experienced? What is unknown?

When I speak of surrender, I am not speaking of indulgence, acting out, or giving in to. I am directing you to the very core of your being. So, what will it be? It is up to you.

The first step then is meditating or just sitting with the desire?

You have already taken the first step by questioning what to do about these desires. In your mature recognition of actions taken toward desire or against desire, you have discovered what these actions have led to. Feeding, indulging, and repressing are directions of the mind outward in an attempt to handle or take care of desires. The direction I am speaking of is inward to the source of the arising—into the fire, through the fire, not feeding it and not putting it out. You go into it to discover what it really is. *Reality* is our concern here. What is this *really*? Who am I *really*?

For this meeting you can have no reference to past thoughts, past activities, or past conclusions. You must be absolutely still. Stillness means all activity of the mind ceases. Then direct experience reveals what is. There is nothing to do.

Just simply stop doing what you have been doing, and then reality is immediate.

Thank you.

• • •

After having experienced awakening and deepening of that awakening, still unconscious habits are manifesting in my life that are harmful or stupid. What to do?

Stop them. Isn't it obvious? Anything that is harmful or stupid, stop right away, immediately. When it is obvious, there is no excuse, and this in itself is the deepening. Don't give yourself any excuses. Be finished with stupidity and harmfulness. When stupidity arises from past actions, past choices, past desires, it is obvious if you are willing for it to be obvious. If you are willing to see, you are willing not to go to sleep to what is harmful and stupid, but to see it, to feel it, to experience the enormous, omni-directional pain of it. It is not just in you or in some other. It is omni-directional.

This is excruciating. It must be excruciating. The willingness for total surrender and sensitivity is the willingness not to allow anything to pass unseen.

You have spent many years denying what is obvious. Our whole culture is built on this denial and deflection. Our subculture in particular, out of some desire for personal freedom and to break out of the bondage of the generation before us, has also spent years denying what is obviously stupid.

Now be still and tell the truth. At this point no one can tell you this truth. No one can tell you to do one particular action and not do some other particular action. It is simply obvious as it arises. No matter what story or justification you are telling yourself, the willingness to see what is stupid reveals the possibility of surrender to what is *not* stupid— pure, eternal intelligence.

You now have the opportunity to totally and fully experience the impulse to either deny the stupidity or to indulge the stupidity by acting it out. This impulse, when it is directly and totally experienced, burns up the stupidity! In this burning, there is, as you say, a deepening. Deeper, always deeper.

You can expect these old habits to arise. They have been fed and nurtured and practiced for a very long time. They know where to get a good meal. You must expect them to show up, and they know how to tug at your heart strings and at your neck. These are the tricks of the mind, but the trickster has been exposed. In awakening there is the realization that either in denying impulses or in following impulses, one continues to sleepwalk.

I am not here to teach you some kind of code of conduct. You don't need me to teach you that, and it has been tried unsuccessfully anyway. The latest code of conduct just has to get shoved aside for the next code of conduct. Realization of who you are is not about a code of conduct. It is simply about recognizing what is obvious and what is stupid. I am speaking of basic maturity.

You are no longer a child, and fulfillment will not be found in the attempt to return to childhood. Recognize and feel the excruciating impulse to act out something very stupid, or to repress that acting out, which is also very stupid. In that simple recognition, there is the great opportunity to directly experience whatever arises. Then even these past impulses, these latent tendencies, this subconscious material, are all the vehicles for deepening in the willingness to burn in surrender.

People often ask me about addictions; the yearning that has with it the impulse to find some substance or some *thing* to quench it. The impulse is itself the yearning for fulfillment. I always counsel to jump directly into the fire of yearning. This jump is neither acting out the impulse nor denying the impulse. In each arising of these impulses, there is the deepest, most profound opportunity to burn away layers of misidentification and suffering.

You know the moments where there is the feeling or the thought, *I must not feel this, or I will go crazy. I must do that. I must have this. If I just have it one more time, then I'll be satiated.*

Stop this sell-out. Even though all of society supports this sell-out, and many people are making fortunes on this sell-out; stop. This is very, very simple. It doesn't need extensive analysis.

This is the challenge of surrender. Whatever you think I mean by surrender, I mean something deeper. Please understand that true surrender is neither repression, nor denial, nor ignoring, nor acting out, nor discharging. Surrender is the willingness to be crucified.

Some impulses are extremely strong. Some of them are biochemical. Some have been practiced and worshiped. In the surrender to the crucifixion of the moment, there is resurrection. As soon as there is total surrender, there is the discovery that when everything is lost, everything is found. The very peace and bliss that you have unsuccessfully been seeking in habitual, harmful activities is realized, not by following the habit, and not by denying the habit, but by being willing to burn in the impulse with no movement of the mind in any direction. Surrender.

• • •

I have heard you speak of resolve. Is there some difference between resolve and surrender?

Total surrender is effortless resolve. Resolve means being willing to see the slightest tendency to turn from truth. Resolve means being surrendered to seeing truth, rather than to seeing things look a certain way. Rather than seeing either enlightenment or ignorance, you are surrendered to simply seeing. Seeing deeper and deeper.

There is always more that you can see, and this is glorious. Glorious! Every instant, life gives you the opportunity for deeper resolve, deeper surrender, deeper humbling. Every instant, in every direction.

That is the glory of limited perception. That is the glory of the conditioned existence. Because you have been conditioned to see things in a certain way, you now have the endless opportunity to see *through* the conditioning. All of the uphill struggling can now pay off.

You may have aeons of latent tendencies and habits of mind that will come calling. Let them come! They are vehicles and gifts for deeper and deeper surrender, deeper humbling, deeper being swept off your feet, being floored. Always you can be more deeply prostrate at the endlessness of truth.

• • •

I keep thinking I've got it; then I land flat on my face. Is there a point or stage where surrender and resolve are finished?

No. Resolve, which *is* surrender, is gloriously necessary as long as there is breath in the body.

I tell you continually that beingness is naturally easy; however, it is only experienced as easy if you are true to Truth. Not if you are true to particular phenomenal displays. Not if you are true to particular biochemical firings. If you are true to phenomena, then you will go the way conditioned existence has been going throughout time. I promise you this. But you don't have to rely on my promise. Simply tell the truth about your own experiences throughout time, and you will see that this is so. It is a hard truth because there is often an infantile idealization of the way things should be.

Hard truth, if met in the resolve to be absolutely true, is nothing. There is no effort. The effort, the struggle, and the experience of landing come from trying to cling to a certain phenomenon, or trying to get something again, or trying to get something someplace else. Whether it is the phenomenon called personal power, or the phenomenon called sexual excitement, or the phenomenon called spiritual power, it is all entrapment by the mind.

There is nothing wrong with phenomena. Some phenomena are quite delightful, and some phenomena are quite horrifying; but all phenomena are simply phenomena. If you attempt to cling to any of it, if you reach or grasp for any of it, you will experience yourself as bound. You will be following the mind, subtly or grossly. The value of satsang appearing in your consciousness again and again over time is to point to this very basic truth.

All the books and all the teachers always say the awakened being is very rare. This may have been true in your past and in the collective past. Whether it remains true in the present and in the future is up to you, now. Self-realization takes a resolve that is so total, it is unknown. When resolve is total, then resolve is ease of being.

Your life, as you live it now, *is* the reflection of what you really want. If what you really resolve is the surrender to truth, then you will live your lifetime in surrender to that, and not to some phenomenal display. If you surrender to the truth that no phenomenon has ever touched, you are free. Your life is then a beacon of freedom. Freedom having nothing to do with comforts or discomforts, likes or dislikes, excitement or dullness. True freedom. The truth of who you are *is* this freedom, and these phenomenal displays are simply masks, clothes, passing clouds, chemical or electrical moments.

The usual or normal pattern is to slip back into trance, to reincarnate into suffering. When what has been cast aside appears in another way, through another door, promising more glory, more beauty, more thrills, the temptation will be to say, "Oh, yes. I've waited for this forever. I'll get back to truth later."

Unswerving resolve is, in fact, the most extraordinary, the most unusual possibility for your life. You have the total support of all awakened Being in all realms throughout time, and still, it is totally up to you. You are supported, you are cheered, you are shaken, you are cajoled, and still it is up to you.

True resolve is the most ruthless act of a lifetime. It is the willingness to die to all hope of pleasure. It is the willingness to surrender to truth. You can't surrender to truth so that you will get some more pleasure. You have of course tried to make that deal, and what you have gotten is more suffering—perhaps with extreme pleasure—but finally, more suffering.

Expect the deepest, most thrilling displays of phenomenal temptation. Expect to arise that which you have hungered for, that which is latent in the most secret recesses of your mind. Whether it is display of personal power, or an appearance of the hungered for soul mate, or the winning of wealth, or some personal recognition, it will present itself because it all lies in wait as subconscious tendencies.

What makes resolve difficult is the attempt to also hold onto some idea of personal gratification. Ironically, this in itself is hell. When you are willing to face whatever temptation, horrible or exquisite, fully and completely, when you are willing to die to all fantasies of personal gratification, you discover gratification as who you are.

Expect to be pushed and pulled and flipped, to be attacked from the side and the back, to be presented with flowers and sweets, and then to be clubbed. This is called Leela, the play of the Self or God's dream. Leela plays very hard. If you are surrendered to truth, then this play will only push you deeper into truth. If you are, in fact, surrendered to some phenomenal experience, you will be pulled out of the experience of your own being as gratification itself and into the search for "more," or "different," or "better," which are the names of hell.

• • •

It seems I've been given a very active mind. It's receiving and checking out so much, so many things, all of the time. There is now a lot of attention being given to my music by a major producer, and this phenomenon you were speaking about is very big. There is "the big album," and all of this attention and touring. I was just happy being here, and now it's, "I'm getting there. I'm gonna get it."

There are many people who have gone before you and fallen into this same trap of fame and money and recognition. Use their fall as the encouragement for unswerving resolve.

Turn the active mind's attention to itself, and see what is discovered. Praise and adoration come and go. Hate and attack come and go. They are meaningless if your attention is on the truth of the bliss that is within you.

A current of bliss will reveal a river of bliss. A river of bliss will flow naturally into an ocean of bliss. An ocean of bliss lifts up into a sky of bliss. The sky of eternal Self is truth. If life presents roses or if it presents ashes, attend to truth. You may like the roses and hate the ashes, but attend to truth.

I notice my mind is attending to all the phenomena that

seem to be occurring in the moment.
What about truth?

Truth seems to be in acknowledging all of the phenomena.

Where has that led you?

It almost seems like a balloon from the mind starts commenting on what certain appearances mean.

This is all imagination. If you attend to truth, you are acknowledging what no phenomena have ever touched. You are acknowledging the truth of your Self. It doesn't mean you hate phenomena, and it doesn't mean you love phenomena. It means you are attending to truth.

Truth is permanent. Phenomena are impermanent. You know this essential distinction from your day to day experience. This is not esoteric. It is very concrete. Phenomena come and go. Thoughts come and go. Emotions come and go. People's responses come and go. Your attitude about yourself comes and goes. Good, bad, up, down, excited, flat; all of that comes and goes. Truth remains present, alive, available, blissful. Attend to truth, and phenomena are simply comings and goings. Not only are they simply comings and goings, but they are actually vehicles for deeper realization of truth.

That's what I was referring to.

Phenomena are not vehicles for deeper realization of truth if you acknowledge phenomena rather than acknowledge truth.

Aren't they one and the same?

Have you realized that phenomena are nothing at all? Otherwise, you are using a spiritual concept to justify following of phenomena and then wondering why you keep suffering.

Using spiritual truth to serve egocentric understanding is a trick of the mind, and I see it in tragic ways. Forget any concept of "one and the same." If you are remembering it, you are using it as justification for following phenomena, and this is the trap.

Forget everything, and in that instant you will see what is permanent. Attend to that. Surrender to that. The mind cannot be busy then. The mind can only be busy with attending to phenomena. In the quieting of the mind, the deepest realization naturally appears because it is already here. In your attendance to phenomena, you overlook what, in fact, you hope phenomena will give you, or what you hope phenomena will keep away.

Surrender is a ruthless, unsentimental cut. The desire for this cut is why people traditionally retreat from the world of phenomena and live the life of a sadhu,[*] or a recluse, or a monk. The world of phenomena that must be left is the world within your own mind. Surrender your interpretations, your measurements, and your qualifications for at least one instant. In that surrender, see what is available. Then you have the opportunity for free choice, for true intention.

I can guarantee you that many people want phenomena, and so they will spend however many lifetimes chasing

[*]   sadhu - Ascetic renunciate.

phenomena. If what you want is truth, then take one instant to let go of everything you thought would give you truth, and experience what is already here. Then and only then do you have real choice.

Is the whole process just surrendering to what is?

Yes, and if you are to surrender to what is, first you must discover what *is*. Do you understand? What *is*, is truth. Truth is permanent, eternal, unchanging presence. If you are surrendering to phenomena and calling phenomena "just what is," then you have played a nasty trick on yourself. Then you have bitten the dog that will bite you back because it looked like something soft and sweet.

I often hear, "Hey, I'm just going with what is, you know. Love the one you're with, right?" We have all tried that in the name of freedom, in the name of truth, in the name of choice, but secretly in the name of, "I've gotta be me."

That is not what *is*. What *is*, is unchanging. All phenomena do arise from that, do exist never separate from that, and do return to that. But in the deep disease of conditioned existence, there has been attention paid only to phenomena, and in that, there is unnecessary suffering.

It is possible to stop unnecessary suffering. Only when truth is realized are phenomena no problem.

We are trained by what we hear people say. If we like what they are saying, if we resonate with the energy or if nice things happen, then when they speak, we want to learn and remember what it is they are saying. We hold in our minds what we think it all must mean, and then we model our concepts after that. That is not what realization is about. Final truth never has been spoken and can never be spoken. What can be spoken, what has been spoken, comes and goes. I am speaking of what *is* in all the comings and goings. This that you truly are, *is*.

If for one instant you surrender to *is*-ness instead of surrendering to phenomena, then you honestly have a choice. It doesn't mean you are any less *is*-ness if you choose to follow phenomena. Maybe you like to suffer. Maybe you like drama more than peace. That is all right at certain stages, but you are here in satsang to discover the possibility of choosing truth—permanent, eternal, never going anywhere, truth.

• • •

I say a lot of things in satsang, but the truth is, I am really only saying one thing in as many different ways as this mind-stream can conjure. What I am saying is simply to trust your Self.

When I say trust your Self, I mean to trust the truth of who you are. For this trust to be complete, you must first discover who you are. You cannot wait any longer, and you cannot rely on someone else's interpretation—mine, your parents', or your government's. You have to discover directly who you are. Then you have the opportunity to trust that discovery totally and completely. To surrender all thoughts, all emotions, all interpretations of reality, and to see what comes from that trust.

Gangaji . . . I surrender.

This declaration is a standing up, a standing away from the herd of self-hatred and self-doubt. Good. Your surrender is eternally accepted and celebrated.

Now, what has been lost in this surrender?

Judgment of others. Judgment of myself.

What has been found?

What has always been here!

That's right! In surrender what is found is what has always been here. Isn't it about time you surrender to what has always been here? What a victory this surrender is.

I see your face opening and tears streaming. I don't know if these words even make sense to you. It doesn't matter. Something recognizes itself and shakes in that recognition. The byproduct of that recognition, the shaking and the tears and the declaration, "I surrender," is a beautiful event.

There is no end to surrender. When you declare, "I surrender," this is the beginning. The gate of surrender is wide open, and you are walking through the gate. Now it begins. What has always been here begins manifesting its eternity in the mind-stream that has surrendered before it.

• • •

I just realized that you are constantly surrendering.

Yes!

That it's not like you arrived anywhere.

I arrived nowhere, and I am finding no limits to this nowhere. Anytime some semblance of arrival appears, I discover it to be nowhere, nothing. Surrender is not something that *happened* to me one day. It is something that *is*.

The great fear of surrender is that some kind of nihilistic force will take over, or some kind of brainwashing will come in, but it is obvious we have all already been brainwashed. That is the nature of conditioned existence.

Are you willing to surrender all conditioning? Not to substitute a new philosophy or a new point of view, but surrender it all, so that that which is before all points of view can be revealed.

It's always new!

That's right. Otherwise realization is something that happened yesterday, in the past. Realization is absolutely new, and at the same time it is seeing that which has always been.

There is no end to surrender, no end to awareness, no end to being, no end to God, no end to truth, no end to who you are.

Exposing the Core of Suffering

Most people are firmly convinced that if they can get rid of their suffering, happiness can be achieved.

We have tried everything to get rid of suffering. We have gone everywhere to get rid of suffering. We have bought everything to get rid of it. We have ingested everything to get rid of it. Finally, when one has tried enough, there arises the possibility of spiritual maturity with the willingness to stop the futile attempt *to get rid of,* and, instead, to actually experience suffering. In that momentous instant, there is the realization of that which is beyond suffering, of that which is untouched by suffering. There is the realization of who one truly is.

• • •

I am a person who has been politically involved most of my life. I am greatly concerned with human rights and fairness and justice. I have had the belief that if the murderous, greedy dictators would just get out of the way, then people could find the way to peace.

Then I came to a satsang where you talked about Self-inquiry. You spoke about turning inwards and focusing on the question, "Who am I?" At that point the lights came on. "Who am I?" appeared everywhere. I see now that there is no solution in focusing on what is "out there." The only possibility for peace is within myself.

When your heart is open, your life is peace. Peace is willing to see everything. Be willing to see fully and completely every impulse of separation and acquisition and greed. Be willing to see hate and war. The promise of this seeing is the end of the war.

When the personal war is ended, "your" life is not limited to the personal anymore. "Your" lifetime is then turned toward peace and reconciliation. Then "your" life is the resolution of these demanding questions of justice and human rights that you have had all your life. Your life is a life given to resolution.

Honor the life that is peace. Bow to the peaceful life. Support the peaceful life. Serve the peaceful life. Anytime, anyplace you feel a wavering, call on all other servants of peace to remind you of what is always peacefully alive within you.

Most people come to spiritual or religious gatherings in search of personal enlightenment. That is how it begins. The lack of personal fulfillment serves as the grit that reveals the self-hatred and the resulting mental/emotional war. By consciously facing suffering without recourse to the infinite strategies of avoidance, by seeing it in all its horror, and being willing to continue to see it as long as it is there, the horror can be finished.

We will see what happens when more people are willing to give up their personal wars. We have seen what has occurred when people are not willing to give them up, when they are only willing to attempt to change others. We have seen this over and over and over.

I am asking you to step away from the herd, to be exposed to all kinds of dangers and lack of safety. I am asking you for an instant of pure meditation, for one second of silence.

The herd is the activity of the mind. To know the peace that is permanently present, you must be willing to experience the exposure.

I want to live this lifetime open and exposed to everything that comes, never wavering in my devotion to peace for all being.

I am happy to hear you speak like this so truly, so clearly. It is time.

• • •

I'm deeply concerned about the fact that twenty percent of the world's population consumes and accounts for eighty percent of the world's natural resources. I'm concerned about the fact that in the next century the world's population is going to double and then quadruple.

Suffering is not limited to a group of people living in poverty or a group of people living in affluence. Suffering is almost universal.

If you are concerned with really getting at the root of the suffering, which, in the case that you describe, is manifested by the overwhelming impulse to consume and acquire, then let us have a dialog. If you are just concerned with saying, "Bad, bad, bad," then your finger-pointing is not different from any pretext for war throughout time. We can study history to see what these pretexts have in fact led to.

So please, tell me, what is it you really want?

Well, I'm concerned about the suffering that those facts end up generating.

If you are just concerned with the suffering that those facts reveal, you are quite possibly overlooking the root of suffering. Getting *this particular* group which is doing that to stop doing that will not touch the root of suffering. As long as the root remains, the suffering will break out again and again.

Well, what do I do with that information?

For a moment, drop all facts about everything. I guarantee you that everywhere you look you can find some fact that points to suffering. It is very tempting to stop at the facts, and then gather more facts around that.

Going for the root of suffering does not excuse the greed and the acquisition and the consumption. But if you stop your investigation at the manifestation of suffering, if you want to merely chop off the fruit or the flower, then the root of suffering grows stronger. You must realize this from history.

Whenever revolution has arisen, even with pure idealism, whether it be political revolution, religious revolution, or ecological revolution, it has failed to eradicate suffering. Finally, the root of suffering must be exposed, and this exposure begins right where you stand.

I am not by any means against commitment to a cause. I am saying before you commit to anything, without pointing outward, discover the root of greed. First discover the root of fear, hate, and aggression. Then whatever cause you champion, you champion from Self-confidence. Then your cause is no more about changing facts and statistics. It is about exposing the root of suffering and revealing the source of happiness.

Thank you. I didn't know at the end of the question if I was really going to understand your answer.

I didn't know either. When there is no knowing what will be said and no knowing what will be understood, there is true speaking. There is true hearing.

I have a small amount of experience being involved in political groups. Once, I even went to jail for nonviolently protesting some action taken by the government. In my involvement, I discovered something interesting. I discovered that the root of most political action is based on making somebody else wrong so that one's own enormous sense of emptiness or incompleteness or wrongfulness does not have to be felt, does not have to be experienced. I discovered within my own mind, and I observed in others, that there was primarily an investment in keeping the struggle going. Ironically, there was more energy directed to the struggle than to the resolution of the struggle.

Unfortunately, this same dynamic is present in most nations, most societies, most cultures, most sub-cultures, most religious groups, most families, and most individuals.

Most action of any kind is an attempt to run from the fear of being nothing. There is the hope that, *If I do this, then I will be something, and this something is worth something. That worth will, at least for a moment, make me forget that perhaps I am really nothing.*

The truth is you really are nothing! Left unexperienced, this *nothing* is terrifying, and frantic mental activity is generated to fill the seeming void of nothingness. The sublime joke and the great discovery is that in the willingness to be nothing, you realize fulfillment; you realize inherent peace. Then there is no need for *them* to do something so that *you* can feel whole. Action that follows fulfillment is pure, spontaneous, creative, and intuitive, having nothing to do with any perceived lack. Commitment is to peace and the overflowing of peace however it overflows—spiritually, politically, through the arts, speaking, and in silence.

Once this discovery has been made, then yes, there can be enlightened politics, enlightened religions, enlightened families, enlightened relationships of all kinds.

The possibility is in this lifetime, in this moment, now, to expose the root of suffering. When the root is exposed to the light of truth it cannot survive. Then the entire tree of *your* suffering is finished. Without the root, it cannot continue.

For many of us in this country of affluence, there is no real necessity to think of the next meal. There is no real necessity to worry about where you will sleep tonight or if someone will gun you down. So, there is no longer any excuse to avoid this essential discovery. If you are distracted from this discovery, you are distracted by trivial matters.

Discover who you are, and let your life be lived from that discovery. Then we will see.

• • •

I have so much trouble accepting the suffering that is going on in the world, and I really wonder if in the state of true love everything is seen as okay.

True acceptance does not condone starvation or hatred or suffering. It sees *through* violent fragmentation to inherent wholeness. That seeing *through* serves the end of starvation or hatred or suffering.

Not just the big suffering, but all the little things too.

Yes, the mundane suffering as well as the profound suffering. True love has as part of its nature infinite compassion for suffering.

When you say, "I have trouble with the suffering, I am suffering because of the suffering," who is this *I*? *Who* is suffering?

Sometimes I fall out of it.

This *I* who falls out of it and falls into it, who is this *I*? Where is this *I*?

In my mind.

Where is this mind? Can you particularize this mind or this *I* as a separate entity? I know you can imagine it that way, but in looking directly at the imagination, is this *I* particularized from the totality of being?

No, it's not.

Excellent. You are not separate from the totality of being, as your toe is not separate from the totality of your body. If your toe hurts, you are aware of your toe hurting. True compassion recognizes the experience of hurting and attends to the hurt as best as possible. If the toe isn't attended in its hurting, it may start to fester, and then maybe the foot or even the leg has to suffer because of inattention.

True understanding does not mean neglect of the world. While your toe is not the totality of your body, it is also not separate from the totality of your body. Change the bandage. Use medicine. With compassion, attend to your true Self however you appear—as other human, other species, as the entire universe.

Compassion is an aspect of love, not a sentimental, judgmental story of love. It is not "bad" toe or "poor" toe or "wrong" toe or "stupid" toe. It is compassionate attention. Love.

• • •

A couple of satsangs ago I asked a question about suffering. I don't remember what you said, but it really made me angry.

That happens sometimes.

What I thought was, "How dare you? How dare you take this away from me, and to take it away so easily!" But you know, I walked out of here with such a lightness. A lightness that I had not ever really felt before. What I have found since then is joy . . . the other side maybe.

I wouldn't say that joy is the other side of suffering. That's really the good news about joy. When you experience joy directly, you find no end to it; you find no limit to it. Even no cause for it! When you experience suffering directly, you find it is not even there. This is *very* good news!

What I have found is that I've become much more available to the world.

Excellent.

I wrote in my journal this morning asking, "Where has this longing gone? This longing that's connected to the suffering." What I wrote was that it has turned into a simple prayer of thanks.

This is so beautiful, so immediate! This is the beginning. Surrender reveals the open mind, and the open mind is freed from the imagination of separation from pure, free consciousness, which is bliss.

I have heard it said that suffering is voluntary, and bliss is involuntary.

I like that! I would add that suffering has cause, and joy is causeless. If you assign a cause to joy, then there is suffering. Realize causeless joy. It is your inherent nature.

I am not speaking of a "la-la, ha-ha-ha" kind of joy. I am speaking of the joy that even allows unhappiness. I am speaking of the joy of being, of the ease of being, of not needing anything, not needing the right circumstance, not needing the preferred state—just pure Being recognizing Itself as consciousness and delighting in Its discovery.

• • •

I come from a background where there is a lot of attention paid to suffering, and this week in satsang I've been very emotional. It has undoubtedly been one of the richest weeks of my life with a lot of pain and grief, incredible joy, and deeper understanding.

One of the things that happened to me that was so amazing was that I saw beyond the suffering to something so much bigger and higher. I don't really know what happened, but I hope I can come back to that. I saw suffering like a cloud, that there is all this light and sky and so much beyond.

This is essential. Before an experience like this, everything spoken in satsang seems abstract or theoretical. In the midst of extreme emotionality, that which is untouched by any emotion revealed itself. You have glimpsed the truth. This glimpse, this perception, is now in memory. Though you cannot get back to the experience, the memory of it is a testimonial.

Don't try to recapture that moment. Something in your personal identity has been cut now. Some identification with feelings or circumstances or emotions as the limit of reality has been cut, and what is limitless has revealed itself.

You cannot get back to your true Self, because you are *already* there. You are where your true Self is.

I am very happy for you. It is a moment of great joy. It is the beautiful death knell of personal identification. A death that is a celebration of that which is deathless.

• • •

I've been in the situation where the Self is answering all my questions. Recently, however, the questions are coming up, but there is no answer. There is only the recurrence of these questions that are demanding an answer, and I notice I want to deny this.

Questions neither touch the true answer nor disturb it in any way. What a wonderful joke. If you deny the question, the question assumes the veil of projected reality. If you follow the question into metaphysical explanation and analysis, it assumes the veil of mental reality. If you give the question to the answer, the question is at rest. Then the question itself has been liberated, has been set free, and is no longer in the hungry ghost realm.

A memory is a hungry ghost, crying for liberation. Release the ghost.

It seems I experience peace, and then there is a sudden return to the suffering, and I wonder, "How did I get back here?"

There is peace, and then in peace, some memory of past suffering arises. Do not close the door of peace by attempting to keep past memory locked in the realm of suffering. Suffering will keep knocking at the door. This is what I mean when I say "hungry ghost."

The moment of peace is an announcement of satsang. Peace welcomes all.

Welcome whatever arises, whatever its disguise, whatever its past association. Expect these past associations, these hungry ghosts, these latent tendencies, to arise. In fact, in your announcement of peace, this is the call for the past to be liberated. There is some past demon in some realm of memory that hears, "Ah, satsang. This is my chance. Maybe now I will be admitted into satsang."

There is almost an effort to stay in no-mind when it arises.

Your effort is the suffering! Recognize that your effort reveals a latent belief that no-mind is something that is not yours now. No-mind is truth now. Everything appears in that. You cannot leave no-mind. You cannot leave your Self.

When one of these latent tendencies or thought forms or demons or hungry ghosts appears, this is the opportunity to discover directly if there are limits to peace, *really*. Not what you have believed the limits to be or what you have imagined has taken you from peace, but really, what are the limits of peace? There is no need to war against your experience of non-peace. Invite everything that arises to peace. That which arises and is welcomed to satsang will either disappear or be revealed, in reality, as peace itself.

• • •

I am really aware of my thoughts, and I judge myself for having them. I'm afraid to give up my judgment of them.

Afraid that you will then be a bad person?

My judgment is that I <u>am</u> a bad person.

We are taught that we are essentially bad, we are essentially savage, and that we must learn to be good. Obviously, there are many things that must be learned, and conditioning itself is no problem. When conditioning is overlaid with the belief that you are essentially bad, there is enormous, unnecessary suffering.

Our parents taught us in this way. Their parents taught them the same way. It is certainly the way our schools teach us. It is the way our politicians speak to us, and it is the consensual belief. You believe that the Buddha is essentially good. You believe that Christ is essentially good. But there is still the belief that *you* are basically bad. You believe this because you have had bad thoughts. You have had negative emotions. You have done bad things. You have proof that you are bad, and you suffer with this proof.

This is the trap, and in that belief, there is a deep unwillingness to uncover the root of the badness. There is an unwillingness to experience the internal violence. There is an unwillingness to directly experience the badness you imagine yourself to be.

I see that every time I judge someone or something it is a thought in my own mind. I recognize that, and I judge the judging.

I am not saying there is anything wrong with judgment. Obviously, judgments are also a part of this play, and if you see something as bad, you must acknowledge you see it as bad. You do not want to get into philosophical numbness. You know there are occasions where you must shout out, "This is bad. This is wrong. Stop!"

What I am addressing is the internal litany that you practice weekly, daily, or hourly. In the avoidance of direct experience, what is felt as bad within your own mind is left untransformed. It is left as some seed of self-hate, some sense of worthlessness. There is a deep-seated belief that you must continually think to do the right thing and then to analyze every act because obviously, if you don't, your badness will slip through.

There is nothing wrong with the intention to stop contributing to the badness of the world, except that it keeps you in your mind. It keeps you judging, and then judging the judgments, and through judgment you perpetuate self-hatred.

Here is the opportunity to open your mind totally to all of the negativity that you have ever acted out or ever thought. Horrible thoughts can arise in the mind, and yes, you must take responsibility for that. To take responsibility is to stop the mental trap of, *I am bad. I shouldn't think that. I've got to practice being good.* Taking responsibility is being willing to really experience the enormous pain of that negativity or hatred. Ruthlessly and non-sentimentally experience the pain. Be still in the core of the pain.

You feel you have done horrible things, hurtful things, mean-spirited things, nasty things, maybe even evil things. Out of your unwillingness to directly experience the hurt of these actions, the tendency to hurt remains hidden in the mind. The tendency festers for a while and then erupts in some negative thought or emotion or action.

Experience the pain. Maybe you haven't been able to before. Maybe as a child you couldn't, you didn't have the resources or the maturity, but now you can. Have the willingness to meet the pain that you have been unwilling to meet.

It is very easy to tell stories of how we have been hurt, but you have hurt at least as much as you have been hurt. And, anyway, it is finally the same hurt.

Feel the suffering that you have caused. Whatever you have done to someone else you have done to yourself, and in denying that, you give suffering power for future suffering. When you experience the pain of the suffering that you have caused, you know without a doubt that you have done it to yourself. This in itself is a revelation. In that, you discover what is underneath the pain.

I tell you that what causes the pain is ignorance. At some time you believed you needed to get something for yourself, and this belief led to greed and lust and hate and violence. In that feeling of need, there is the germ, the kernel, of Self-yearning. When you are willing to experience it all the way to the core, you will see that all this hurt that was done to you, and that you have done to others, has all been based on igno-rance. It has been based on the mistaken misconception that, *I am not*. Experience *not-ness* to realize, *I am*. *I am* is pure, untainted, sattvic* being, naturally cleansed of the past in its own Self-recognition. It is the doorway to Self-realization. Self is nothing that can be purified for it is nothing that can be dirtied.

To keep the door open to meet one's karma, to meet one's subconscious beliefs, to experience them all fully, is to release the past and offer it freedom.

• • •

I see people who are pretending to be open and have fun when they are really suffering.

---

* sattvic - Pure, tranquil, reflection of Truth.

Yes, this pretense is denial of suffering, and pretense itself is suffering. Both the denial of suffering and the entertaining of suffering lead to more suffering. I am not speaking of putting on a happy face. I am speaking of no face. Then you do see falseness. You do see pretense. You do see suffering. And, more importantly, you see what is forever deeper than pretense or suffering. You see natural goodness shining through all the masks of suffering.

Do you catch this?

The doubts come in.

When doubts come, invite doubts to doubtlessness. The secret is not to try to overcome doubts or to indulge them, push them aside or deny them. Invite them to satsang, and then you will see the particular habit of doubting, and more importantly, what is at the root of doubting.

Inviting doubt into the limitless truth of being is a way of recognizing vastness, of being no-body. In the vastness, in totality, the suffering of another is not separate from your suffering. It appears in you.

I doubt that I am strong enough or big enough to discover what you suggest.

Your doubt is your slave collar. Unlock the slave collar by questioning who it is that needs to be big and strong. Now, as we meet.

Now?

57

Yes. Now. *Who* is not big enough or strong enough?

(after some time)
There is no one—just space—just vastness.

Where is doubt in this?

Nowhere.

• • •

Gangaji, it seems that I can use the experience of separation like a guidepost to how I'm really connecting with "I Am."

Yes! This is the dharma bell ringing. If there is an experience of separation, if there is an experience of suffering, of holding onto or rejecting pain, you can ask yourself, *What is really going on here? Who is suffering? Who is separate?* Then the experience and perception of duality, the illusion itself, are vehicles that point to truth. Nothing needs to be rejected. If the experience of separation arises, it too can drive you deeper into the truth that is before and beyond any idea of separation or union.

• • •

Will you speak on the distinction between pain and suffering and the role of suffering on the path to enlightenment?

Pain is simply pain, sensations in the physical or emotional body. Suffering is in time and has with it some story line about the pain. The story line generates strands and permutations—who caused the pain, why, when, how, and on and on. There can be an enormous investment in the story, and therefore, a reluctance to let it all go. If you were to let it go, it would mean that all those hours, all those years, all those lifetimes with the preoccupation of "What about me?" would be finished. Finished, with no return on the investment. All of the story gets its life force from this resistance to letting it go.

When the story of pain is released, pain can be experienced as it is.

How do I let the story go?

Open the mind to experience. Experience whatever comes up without filtering or judging. As the mind is opened, concepts are dropped. Opening the mind to pain, or any other physical, emotional, or mental phenomenon, can reveal what is at the core of all phenomena. Pain, experienced with no story line, reveals Buddha nature.

Suffering reveals nothing except more story about pain. Suffering is justification, blame, sentimentalizing, and dramatization of pain.

By opening the mind, pain is discovered to be no thing. This no thing that appeared as pain is absolute. It is intelligence, clarity, joy, and peace. The truth of your Self is discovered in the core of pain. Pain is potentially a vehicle for revealing truth. If the story of the pain is followed, the vehicle is overlooked, and then pain is wasted as more investment in unnecessary suffering.

Certainly all of us have experienced pain of one kind or another—emotional pain and physical pain, personal pain and worldly pain. If you have had the experience of surrendering in the moment that pain arises, not resisting it but actually opening, then you have discovered peace in the midst of pain. In this discovery, you are no longer preoccupied with personal suffering.

You see that when there is an end to personal suffering, you are willing to experience pain beyond any idea of "your" pain. You are willing to experience your neighbor's pain, your parent's pain, your children's pain, the pain of the whole universe, and in that, there is less denial of pain, less dramatization of pain. Then the thoughts circulating around avoidance of pain and the acquisition of agents of pleasure (in the hope of some insurance from pain) lose their power. When you are willing to open, you are willing *to be* fully. Then pain is to be bowed to as simply the satguru appearing as pain, as truth appearing as pain, as God appearing as pain.

This opportunity is available to everyone.

• • •

I definitely know now that I'm not this body, yet I have a problem with migraine headaches. I still want that pain to go away.

Well, stop wanting it to go away.

I've done that too.

What you have done is to stop wanting the pain to go away so that it would go away!

You're right, but nothing works.

Have you tried letting the pain be?

What I've gotten to now is that I can still be joyful and alive and wonderful even with a headache. But I still hate the pain. It hurts, and it does kind of get in the way.

Many bodies have conditions that hurt. Some bodies hurt more than other bodies. If you experience hurt totally, you discover that which is closer than the body, closer than the hurt. Rest in that. The pain comes, the pain goes, you rest in that which is closer. Don't struggle any more with trying to do something with pain. Tend the body, but if your body will not be tended with its migraines, rest in that which does not come and go. Give up the struggle.

The body will have better days and worse days. This is the nature of bodies. But that which doesn't go away has no judgment of good days and bad days.

Rest in that where there is no judgment. Especially on a bad day of the body, rest in that. Then you will see. Without looking for it you will see that even pain has beauty. Even that which you hate, at its core, is beauty.

One day you may even thank this gift. You may say, "I am grateful for this gift that has forced me to see in pain what I imagined was someplace else." If you imagine that truth is only present in good physical feeling or good emotional feeling, that is a limited truth.

There was a time when Ramana's body was being eaten by vermin. There is a point when your body will be eaten by maggots and vermin. Before that time arises, discover your Self not to be limited to your body. You are not separate from your body, and you are not limited to it. Discover immediately, instantly, what is eternal. Not by doing anything but by just being. Discover if there are limits to being.

• • •

Pain seems like a very strong energy. It is almost like bliss.

When you know the core of pain, you know the secret of pain. In that instant, you know bliss. There is only the core there. Everything else is imaginary.

• • •

What do I do when pain or body sensations come again and again?

Do you hold the notion that pain shouldn't come again? When this thought is seen and finished, where is the record of pain coming and going?

Awareness is the record.

Does awareness have the judgment of, "Oh no, not again"?
Well, no.

Pain is pain, and in itself is no problem. You have somehow been taught that you have to escape pain. Aversion to
pain is deeply embedded in the DNA, in the genetic code. Can
you give up what you have been taught about pain?

Pain is just a thought?

It is a word defining a range of sensation from slightly
uncomfortable to horribly intense. For a moment, let's keep
the definition. Let the definition be a useful vehicle in the
dynamic of pain versus pleasure. To cut this dynamic, for an
instant, *be* pain. Be that which you are running from.

Then meeting pain is a skillful means. Isn't that interesting? Your biggest enemy turns out to be your great ally. It has
been calling you, calling you, all these years chasing you no
matter what you did. Clearly there is some message being
announced. Hear the message by being the messenger.

*The Lakota Indian sun dance creates that experience of
renouncing the pain.*

Renunciation has been practiced in many religious orders.
Renunciation often takes the form of self-flagellation. What I
am speaking of is different from renunciation. I am not speaking of dramatizing or amping up the pain, and I am not
speaking of overcoming the pain as in dissociation.

I am speaking of something more subtle. I am suggesting

that you experience pain at its core. I am inviting you to discover what is revealed when physical or psychological pain is not fought or dramatized. When no strategy is followed, you discover what exists at the very core.

You have tortured yourself mentally and emotionally for a long time. Now turn to that tormentor and see who is there.

• • •

I had a powerful experience with Papaji two years ago. It was the most beautiful experience I've ever had, but afterwards it didn't come again. I tried this way and that way. I also tried not trying, but nothing helped me.

Last year I suffered a lot and felt that the hangover from this enlightenment experience was really too much.

So, where does all that leave you?

Here.

Good. This is the place to be. Recognize all of your conclusions about that experience to be in the past, and recognition points you here. Now, be here. Forget about any experience of anything, good or bad.

I don't want to suffer.

When you make this statement, "I don't want to suffer," you are suffering. As long as you say, "I don't want to suffer," you will suffer.

I don't understand.

If everything, even the deepest, darkest suffering, is experienced as it is, you are freed from the twin illusions of escape and safety. As long as there is an unwillingness to suffer, there is endless searching for escape and safety, endless suffering.

This you must understand, and you eventually will. You have rejected suffering, and you have run from this shadow and that shadow. Finally you will say, "Well it's not working. I can want not to suffer over and over, and still I am suffering." In wanting not to suffer, your attention is on suffering. In wanting truth, in wanting freedom, in wanting to be here where you are, attention is placed on truth, freedom, and now. By not wanting to lose an experience, you lose it because your attention is placed on holding rather than experiencing.

The nature of all experience is to appear and disappear. Even the best experiences come and go, but the source of all experiences is present always.

For some instant in your meeting with Papaji, somehow the clinging to any idea of what should be, or what was, evaporated. From that instant, an exquisite, sensory byproduct arose, and you became infatuated with the byproduct. It felt very good. When it passed, as all experiences pass, you began to attempt to get it back. You discovered that grasping for the experience didn't work.

The truth is that when your desire is for truth, and you are willing to realize truth, you will open your heart totally to all of suffering. You will open to your personal suffering, your wife's suffering, your country's suffering, the suffering of the whole cosmos. This is a conscious opening of the heart. You say, "I will not run."

Do not open your heart to suffering so that you will not have to suffer. Do not open your heart to suffering so that you can dramatize yourself as a sufferer. Just be willing to be here where you are. When suffering arises, don't run from it, don't cling to it, don't deny it, don't repress it, don't indulge it, don't act it out. If your mind can direct none of these actions, where is suffering?

It is simple beyond belief, but it is not simplistic. All the past complications of your life, and your wife's life, and your neighbor's life, and your country's life, and humanity's life, and cosmic life arise in this simplicity. In the willingness to discover, even in suffering, what is at the core, you discover what is beyond and closer than any experience. This discovery is what the words enlightenment and freedom point to. It is what can never be practiced, learned, or believed, because it is beyond and closer than any concept or idea in the mind.

What has happened to you is very important, but I caution you not to make a foolish conclusion from this experience.

I was merely looking for another way to experience enlightenment again, but without so much suffering.

There will always be another way. You can endlessly think, *I'll find another teacher. I'll find another country. I'll find another spot in nature. I'll find another lover. I'll find another job. I'll have another child. I'll get rid of this body. I'll take another body!* You will think of many, various strategies until finally, just as the Buddha did, you will say, *I will not move from here. I have tried all doctrines, all practices, all modes, and I find them all limited.* Perhaps they all help at a certain stage, but finally, you refuse to move, you must be still.

If suffering comes, let suffering come. If suffering comes for a million years, let it come. In the willingness to let suffering come, a most extraordinary discovery reveals itself.

You are free. You are free to suffer endlessly, and you are free to stop. You are free to be here, unmoving, unflinching, neither denying nor indulging. You are free to be here absolutely and to discover the depths of here, the measurelessness of here. You are free to discover that when suffering is swallowed in Self, suffering itself becomes a celebration of freedom. The great, feared demon suffering is realized to be a manifestation of truth.

You must be willing to meet suffering in the dead of night, alone and forsaken. Forsaken in your mind by God, guru, society, and life. Forsaken in the dark of the night, in this era, the Kali Yuga, the "dark night." It is your opportunity, in this dark age, to meet this. It is the best of times for this meeting.

Once Papaji said, "Even if you have to go to hell to give satsang, you go, because in hell, satsang is appreciated, satsang can be heard."

Call suffering hell. Call suffering by whatever name you have given it. Meet it. Don't flinch, don't move, don't turn your face. You will discover in the core of suffering, pure, empty intelligence. Then you will recognize and embrace everything as that purity. Nothing is excluded—so-called

YOU ARE THAT!

ugly, so-called beautiful, so-called ordinary, or so-called extraordinary. Until then you are just chasing an idea of *better*. If you are in satsang, then somehow the grace of Ramana and Ramana's awakening through Papaji has reached you. Somehow, mysterious grace has plucked you out to have these words and this presence revealed to you.

Hear this. It is given to you freely, no credentials asked. Ready or not, it is given to you. You are free to drink of it in unbelievable depth, and you are also free to cast it aside. The guru reveals the flame of the truth of Self. Ignition is the guru's gift. That ignition has taken place. It is your Self that is given—by your Self and to your Self—your true Self.

Direct Experience Reveals Self

The projecting power of mind produces the body of mind—mental body, emotional body, physical body, and circumstantial body. By perceptive consensus, these "bodies" are accepted as reality. Through Self-inquiry—*Who am I?*—the thought *I*, or personal trance of reality conceived in the mental body, is revealed to be nonexistent. It is experienced as real, yet it is realized to be unreal—as a play or a movie is experienced as real, yet realized to be *just* a play or movie.

Science has shown that when physical phenomena are investigated very closely, they are revealed to be not as they are perceived to be. Self-inquiry is spiritual investigation of what is perceived to be real—"me," "my story." Spiritual investigation reveals perception of an entity separate from the totality of consciousness to be false perception. Spiritual investigation reveals Self as limitless Being, in truth unbound by any and all perceptions of bondage.

Circumstances rely on physical, mental, and emotional bodies for their perceived existence. How can circumstances be considered real when their components are recognized to be essentially nonexistent?

Paradoxically, in exquisite irony, by recognizing the essential unreality of what has been perceived as reality, there is a momentous release of deep love and compassion for all that is perceived!

By recognizing that which *is* real as oneself, the *experience* of life is totally altered. Altered not by the attempt to alter, but by surrender to that unalterableness revealing itself in all guises of thought, emotion, and circumstance. Altered not by the cultivation of love and compassion, but by the discovery that what is revealed at the core radiates love and compassion. Unimagined, unsentimental love is pulling one deeper into its embrace through all experience.

The question, *Who am I?* experienced directly, reveals the truth at the core of all form—all mental form, all emotional form, all physical form, and all circumstantial form. The core is eternally present, regardless of body, regardless of experience. The core is the presence of Being, radiating intelligence and joy of Itself.

• • •

How do I discover the core of all Being?

For direct Self-inquiry, do not be distracted by the periphery, which is the story or the energetic field of phenomena.

Your story about sadness or any phenomenon is based on

your ancestors' experience, your culture's experience, or your personal history. Your story is unreliable because it is based on a conditioned outlook.

You know that past conclusions are unreliable because they can change so quickly. From the very obvious example of a mirage in the desert to thinking someone is your friend when they are not your friend, or thinking someone is your enemy when they are not your enemy. Thinking one day you are brilliant, and the next day you are stupid. Understand that these stories all come from conditioning.

Everyone is searching for that which is absolutely reliable. Absolute reliability can be discovered because it exists as the core of all phenomena, whether it be physical phenomena—your body; mental phenomena—the *I* thought; emotional phenomena—some feeling; or circumstantial phenomena—some event.

To discover the absolute core of any state, be absolutely still as a state appears or disappears. Be unmoving. When the conditioned tendencies to move away from a state or toward a state arise, relax your mind. Surrender the activity of mind to what is before and after all activity of mind.

• • •

Surrender is new for me. As I surrender I find that my sadness is one of the things I hold on to most tightly. I've practiced sadness for a long time, and I'm afraid to leave it behind. I'm afraid as I surrender I might not have that sadness to give import to me and what I do.

Yes, that is accurate. You won't.

I'll miss it.

Are you sure?

I'm not sure.

I don't believe that you will.

It takes some courage to leave it behind.

It takes the courage to be free. It takes the courage to leave behind what was known, how you have defined yourself and how you have defended that definition. With sadness you might have said, "Ah, this is deep. This is not trivial."

The sadness isn't deep?

No, and if you are willing to directly experience the sadness, you will discover that even the sadness is not sadness! Leave behind the story of sadness. When sadness appears, fully experience it. Do not act it out. Do not discharge it. Do not repress it. Do not deny it. Take none of those usual actions, and simply, without commentary, directly experience sadness.

Please, bring some sadness here and we will examine it. Can you imagine something that makes you sad?

I have some sadness.

Good. Just let it grow for a minute.

I'm good at it. I worship it.

Yes, I understand. Now we want to see what it is that you have so faithfully worshipped. While you are sitting here, stop all of the story line about sadness. Now, where is it? Do you feel it somewhere?

I have trouble finding it without the story.

Yes! But maybe it is hidden somewhere in the subconscious where the story is not even verbalized. It has been told so long that maybe it is embedded on a cellular level or experienced as some weight. Are you aware of that?

Yes.

Now, with consciousness devoid of commentary, go into the core of sadness. Don't try to get rid of sadness. Just experience what exists at the core.

It makes me laugh.

It makes you laugh! Now isn't that interesting? Are you sure?

It makes me laugh.

Good. This is the proper use of sadness. Do you understand now?

I know it, but I don't understand it.

I am pointing you toward direct experience. Most people think that if they are feeling an emotion, they *are* directly experiencing it. Usually, just feeling sadness is actually hovering around the drama of sadness, the story of sadness. Without any mental action taken to deny, discharge, or indulge, plunge directly, totally, into the core of sadness or *anything*, and tell me what is revealed.

Direct experience is great good news. It is the promise of all the Buddhas. It is the promise of Christ. It is the promise of everyone who has ever directly experienced emotional phenomena. At the core of every supposed emotion or event or physical manifestation is . . . well, you experience it and tell me, what is at the core? I tell you all the time.

• • •

I want to understand the difference between the emotional pain that is, and the pain that is unnecessary.

Experience the pain that you perceive to be. Experience it directly, completely, absolutely, holding nothing back. Now, in this experience, speak.

It is the fear of a small child being hurt again.

That child is gone. Don't believe that there is some little child walking around in your chest. The inner-child image can be useful at a certain stage, but remember, it is only an image. It is all in the mind. It is obviously important to release any denial of painful, childhood experiences, but if you just substitute a belief in the reality of a little child imprisoned in your chest, then you continue to wander in illusion and attempt to protect what is nonexistent. Release her. Let her be free. True release comes from the willingness to experience pain completely, absolutely, right now.

You are not a little child. You are not even a woman or a man. Drop that story too. Be as you are, not knowing or imagining what that is.

The mental tendency is to get into some story about feeling. There is some memory, and then either a recoiling from that memory or a kind of sentimental wallowing in that memory, right?

Yes.

It is not necessary.

I've been seeing the obsession so strongly lately.

Wonderful. Seeing obsessive suffering means you are ready. Obsessive thinking is an avoidance of the direct experience of what you fear. Perhaps you are still avoiding hurt carried over from some earlier time in this life-stream. Face that hurt now.

I am right here with you. All the Buddhas of all realms are always with you whenever there is the desire to stop and discover the truth of what *really* is. All helpers known and unknown are right here with you because they are all your own Self recognizing Itself.

Now, without the story, directly experience the core of hurt.

How many times have I been through this? How many people know me, "The Sufferer"?

"You the Sufferer" is the story. That story is either being wallowed in or rejected. Let go of the story that you believe to be real entitled, "Me the Sufferer." Drop the "sufferer," drop the "me," and tell me *really*, what is there?

I see having hoped and suffered, risen and fallen, a million times.

You haven't dropped the story yet. I am not speaking about rising and falling, inflation and deflation. I am speaking of directly experiencing this particular so-called entity, "The hurt one." Where is this sufferer? What is it? When you face it, without the story about it, can you find it?

It feels like a shell, like an armoring.

From the core of this feeling, tell me what is the *reality* of the shell, of the armor.

In order to experience anything directly, you must stop thinking about it. Otherwise, it continues as an indirect experience. Indirect experience continues only with the support of thought in the form of commentary, evaluation, speculation, etc.

What I know is that I feel the hurting inside. It's like a holding on.

Experience the hurting. Go deeper into the hurt itself. Not to get rid of it—there is no need to get rid of the hurt. There is no need to overcome it. There is no need even to be finished with it. Simply investigate, what *is* it?

Well, it has been . . .

We are not speaking of "has been." We are speaking of right now. Be willing to *be* that hurt, so that the hurt is total, and there is no hope of ever escaping the hurt.

I feel the shame of so many people having wanted to see me better, finally.

This is a sidetrack. This is a sentimental story.

It's connected to the center.

This story is a strategy to avoid the center. Surrender to direct experience. Let yourself be finally, absolutely, totally hurt.

Great traditions have arisen in different times all over the planet. One tradition in the West is the psychological tradition. It has many uses, and it has many abuses. Psychology can take you, as all traditions can take you, to the edge. From there, you must leave it behind, unless you want to continually loop through images and thoughts about the past. Pay your respects to the psychological tradition. It has served you well. Now just for an instant, leave it behind.

I feel the hurt as some denial.

Denial takes many forms, and in your particular story it has taken the form of, "Poor Me." There may be horrible experiences around that story. I am not denying your experiences of suffering. I am saying if you will meet the hurt rather than continue to tell the story of suffering, there is the most unbelievable, unimagined revelation alive in the core of hurt. This revelation is also present in the core of fear and in the core of all other modes of suffering. It is in the core of everything.

There's great feeling in the hurt. There's—

Stop. This is a mental trap entitled, "Great Feeling and the Great Love Affair with Great Feeling." You may think feeling is very deep, but the vastness revealed through direct experience is inconceivable. It is revealed in the willingness not to get caught up in the old familiar relationship with feeling. I am not saying to deny feeling. There is nothing wrong with feeling. Just don't set up another story around it.

The dilemma is in the identification of yourself as a feeling person, as a hurt person, as a wounded child. You are not that, and the only way you can recognize fully and completely you are not that is to *be* that, to not resist or run from the hurt—to not run from the fear that this wounded child will always be there, will always be wounded, and to not wallow in the story of the wounded child. Turn and see, what is this wound? Where is it? *Who is wounded?*

I have someone who says to me all the time, "You could let go of it in one instant."

You *can* let it go in an instant. You don't need to think another thought about it. That is the truth. There is no more discussion needed. How many times have you replayed it? How many times have you squeezed it and milked it?

But that letting go in an instant seems other than going into it.

It is the same. All you are letting go of is the story, and when you let go of the story, you discover the true nature of this wound. You discover directly, first hand, the true nature of not only this wound but of all phenomena.

When I go into the hurt and the fear, I really feel they come from not knowing who I am.

Now you have come up with a theory about hurt and fear. I am not interested in theories at this moment. You must leave behind all theories of why this hurt is or what this hurt is. Just experience hurt itself. Discover what exists in the core of it.

There! In that instant, you were realizing it. Then there was some reincarnation of the story around it. I know what is discovered is unbelievable. I appreciate that. What I am speaking of cannot be believed. It is not in any belief system. It is not mapped. Speak from that recognition.

In my experience, I would call it an openness or an acceptance of pain.

When you accept and open to pain, what is pain? What is revealed to be at the core?

Oneness.

When you accept or meet oneness, what is there?

Nothingness.

And when you meet nothingness? Don't even make a story of nothingness.

I'm not contacting the pain.

This *I* itself that is not contacting the pain, what is that? Where is that? Who is that?

I don't know.

Well, find it. Where is this *I?* You made the statement, "I am not contacting the pain." Just roll that statement back . . . pain . . . not . . . contacting . . . am . . . *I.*

What is the experience of this instant when there is no speculation, no theory, no explanation, no conclusion?

Happiness.

Yes! Discovered in an instant. Discovered not by reaching for happiness, nor by running from unhappiness.

There is joy!

Yes, naturally. Now, directly experience happiness. Go deeper. To "go deeper" really means not to follow any story, any commentary.

The great secret discovered when you directly experience the so-called negative emotions—which may seem endless, limitless—is that not only are they not limitless, they are not even really there. What a discovery! Then of course bliss arises, and there may be fear to experience bliss because you want it to really be there. When you directly experience bliss, which does not mean holding onto it and does not mean rejecting it, you discover the bliss that is limitlessness. It does not go away. This is your true nature. The rest is false nature, imitation of nature, perceived nature.

Direct experience is a penetration *through* what has been imitated, what has been believed, and what has been perceived, to what is true. This is the good news of awakening.

• • •

When I think of raising my hand, fear arises. Last satsang it was just really immense. I went to the fear and stayed with it, and it just hovered there. The fear didn't go away, and I don't think I really know what's beneath it, what's at the core of it.

That's right. You have yet to directly experience it. As you say, you are just hovering around it. Even if you say, "I am with it," there is still "me" and "my fear." "I see it. I feel it. I sense it." Fear is then experienced as an object. What I am suggesting is that you leave this *I* behind, and then there is only this thing called fear. See what it really is when there is no one who has it.

This is effortless. I am not saying to push yourself into it. I am not talking about getting rid of fear. I am not interested in your getting rid of fear. Attempting to get rid of is a very old strategy, and it doesn't work. I am talking about realizing the truth of what fear is, or sadness is, or despair is, or what any *thing* is.

There is no need to get rid of anything. Once you recognize the truth of everything, what is there to get rid of?

• • •

I don't want to feel this numbness that I feel, this lifelessness.

In your resistance to numbness, isn't numbness perpetuated? This is where you have to be wise now. Feel numb and lifeless whether you want to or not. Not wanting to feel it hasn't worked. Making war on what we don't like hasn't worked, has it? Attacking it, trying to drive it away hasn't worked. Surely there is enough wisdom to see that.

I feel on the one hand I invite it, and on the other hand I don't. I know that the point is to really feel it, but I'm so afraid of it.

Be the fear. Move out of intellectual understanding. Move out of the intellectual speculation of what the outcome will be. Be willing just to be here, and if resistance is here, it too is welcome. This is the natural course of wisdom.

Trust that which keeps you from bolting, from running away, from leaving. It is bigger than the resistance, and it has no problem with the resistance. Someone told you that you shouldn't be resistant. Someone told you that it is bad to be resistant. Forget that. Resistance has a right to be. Let it have a right to be, and then see. See how happy resistance is to be liberated.

I think there's a lot of juice in resistance.

Find the resistance. You cannot find it by thinking about it. You have thought about it, analyzed it, speculated on it, and made many conclusions. Finally, experience it first hand. You have tried resisting it, running from it, denying it, and numbing out around it. Don't try anything, and see what is there.

That is all I am ever saying in satsang. Don't try anything, and see what doesn't need trying to be. See what already is.

• • •

Ever since the first time I saw you on video, I've been hopelessly lost. I feel like I've come to the end of the rope.

Wonderful! When you are at the end of the rope, you have to throw the rope away. Then you know for certain that the rope was a figment of your imagination.

I don't know how to throw the rope away.

Simply stop holding on. If you are really, hopelessly lost, then instantly you are found. It is only when you can give up the last shred of hope of being found that you can recognize, **I am here.**
Who is lost?

No one. I mean, there is only . . . I can't say it.

Well, you just did. There is no *I* that is lost. This presupposed, lost *I* is false.
You feel lost, and you have thoughts of being lost, or conclusions of being "at the end of the rope," but when you check, when you turn toward the *I* who is lost, you can find no one lost.

Yes, it's true. But more and more there is the experience of being lost, and I just feel ever more desperate.

Find *who* is feeling desperate. The feeling of desperation only continues because you assume that you are, in fact, something that the feeling is hooked on to. And you don't like the feeling. It doesn't feel good. There is the experience of hurting. There is the experience of suffering. There is the experience of being lost.

I understand this is a terrible experience, this experience of being separate. Now check *who* is lost. Find the *I* that you imagine to be lost, and shout out the truth.

Well, I can say the truth, but it doesn't—

Say the truth. You spend so much time saying the lie, now, say the truth. We are so totally conditioned and supported in saying the lie. At least once, say the truth.

I am free . . . but it feels like—

Find the *I* who is free. Then you will be done with both "lost" and "free." Then you will recognize that feelings and states come and go in this truth of *I* that cannot be found any place and cannot be absent from any place. If you cling to *I am free*, then every time the feeling *I am lost* appears, you will fall into self-doubt.

I am free is good medicine for *I am lost*. Now let them both be finished. Then you can just say, "I AM."

It just sounds too much like an affirmation: "I am free, I am free, I am free."

Yes. That is exactly what I just said.

You have lived in denial saying, "I am lost. I am lost. I am lost." Then a beautiful affirmation arises: "I am free. I am free." Oh, what a feeling! Now, bring them together. Who is lost? Who is free? Can you find the one who is lost? Can you find the one who is free?

There is only . . . (silence)

Yes, it's very good that you cannot even attempt to put that into a word.

Direct Self-inquiry is the gift of Ramana. It cuts through all denial and all affirmation.

If you cry out, "I am unenlightened," Ramana asks, "*Who* is unenlightened?" If you cry out, "I am enlightened," Ramana asks, "*Who* is enlightened?" There you will find no thing at all, free of both bondage and enlightenment. Free of whatever feeling arises. Free of whatever thought passes through. Free. It is a freedom that has nothing to do with bondage. Only relative freedom has to do with bondage. Absolute freedom is untouched by relative freedom or relative bondage, and you are That.

• • •

The past two weeks I've been here in Kathmandu I've been totally confused. It's been a real whirlwind of emotions. Everything has just hit me in the face, and it's ridiculous. Sometimes I'm crying all the time. Sometimes I'm laughing. Everything just seems so intense in the moment.

In this moment?

It's beautiful in this moment.

Good. Let's not forget that, please. It is very easy to focus on the past—"I was crying. I was moaning. I was confused." I am not saying to blank out on the past. Obviously, you can learn from the past. Primarily you learn it passed. You learn that even in the midst of confusion or suffering or tears, there was a presence that did not pass, that *is* present.

It's exactly the same presence, only confusion's still there.

Yes, the presence is the same. The presence is continual. This is the truth, and the continuance of presence must be realized. Presence is permanent. Experiences of joy or experiences of unhappiness are overlaid on that presence. Experiences of confusion or experiences of clarity are overlaid on pure presence. Presence is not an experience. It is bigger than the mind. It is bigger than the emotions. It is bigger than the circumstances. Presence is always present. About this, there can be no confusion.

Let confusion come to partake of this presence. Let the confusion of aeons come into this presence. Welcome confusion to satsang. Once you recognize that presence is here, and that it is continual, this is an announcement: "Satsang is being given here." This announcement goes out into the airwaves, and it attracts confusion, fear, and doubt.

It's a big magnet.

Yes. When you recognize that you are presence, confusion and fear and doubt are set free.

What satsang points to is the perpetual, continual, presence of truth. Whenever satsang reveals itself, it opens the door to that which must be liberated. It is not your Self that must be liberated. Your Self is already inherently liberated. It is the ideas that have been imposed on that Self which must be set free.

I still feel that I'd like to get rid of my fear.

To get rid of fear, stop trying to get rid of fear. The experience of fear is the experience of some kind of force, isn't it? Usually there are all kinds of strategies to deal with this force. To be strong in the face of fear, or to try and run from fear, but no strategy works because fear is still believed to be some entity, some power. Eventually there is a moment when you say, "Okay, I am not moving. Come in, fear. Who are you? What are you?" In this moment, as you sit here, are you aware of fear?

At this moment, I am in control of fear.

Then invite some.

I can if I see a tiger right here or something.

With a tiger in the room, appropriately there is an instinctual body fear. I am not saying to get rid of instinctive fear. If there is a bus coming down the road and you have a sense of fear because it is swerving, then yes, listen to that. There is nothing wrong with that. When fear is appropriate, it is your servant. I am speaking of psychological fears that are inappropriate—recurring nightmares, recurring mental torment. Fear that runs your life is inappropriate.

Inappropriate fear is a psychic force which is given great power by the mind in the attempt to run from it or overcome it. There comes a certain point in the dark night where finally you must know what is the reality of this fear that seems to have you by the throat. When the nightmare is directly examined, the tiger is discovered to have no substance. It is just the workings of the mind.

There's great strength in fear.

Yes, you experience great strength in fear, enormous strength. I am not making light of the strength of illusion. Start with the first intimation of fear, when it is just a small ghost. Fear only accumulates strength as you turn from it and put your mental powers into avoiding it, into struggling with it, or into fearing the fear.

The beginning is always the easiest moment. Ask, "What is this really? Who is fearing what?" That kind of questioning in itself is the opening. Questioning the experience of fear is an experience of willingness not to run from it.

I know fear seems to have enormous power, but this is only power that you have given it. Fear is nothing without that power. In the direct experience of fear, its power is finished.

It is the same with any suffering—despair, anger, or any of the other so-called negative emotions that entangle the mind. Meet any emotion at its beginning. I am saying to neither express nor indulge it. Simply meet it in stillness.

You may feel like you are being shaken and torn apart, but in the willingness to remain still, you will recognize what are shaken and torn apart are the defenses of the mind. You will recognize that in the core of fear is limitless, joyful intelligence: Sat-Chit-Ananda.[*] It is not usually recognized in the periphery because there is so much mind activity, but when you sink right into the core, Sat-Chit-Ananda is revealed.

Your realization through small fears will encourage you to meet bigger fears. Then, face the final fear. The fear that it is possible not to exist—the fear of death. Fear of death is based on the belief that you are limited to your body. You know very well that it is possible for the body not to exist. Death of the body moves closer and closer every moment. When you are willing to face the fear of nonexistence, you discover what existence is. You discover *who* existence is. You discover your Self. Then fear, suffering, and even death are your allies.

Hinduism depicts Shiva with a cobra around his neck. In this image the most dreaded fear is portrayed as the ally. May your fear be revealed as your ally, your call to that which is both forever beyond fear and forever the truth at the core of fear.

• • •

I feel panic, and I'm afraid of this panic.

Panic is a certain kind of very fast vibration of fear.

It's the fear of not being able to do anything.

---

[*] Sat - True Beingness.
Chit - Intelligence aware of Itself as True Beingness.
Ananda - Supreme bliss of Self-recognition.

I am not counseling you how to overcome panic. It doesn't need to be overcome. I am directing you to discover what is in the core of fear or panic.

I am directing you right into the center of this that you are fearing. In order to experience the core, simply stop all definition and evaluation.

Where are you experiencing this panic? Where is it located?

In the body.

Is it radiating? Where is the source of it?

I feel rigid.

Like frozen? Like your body is frozen rigid?

Yes.

Psychological fear has been habitually avoided. It is possible to face it fully and completely with your mind open. If you attempt to face fear bringing along concepts of what you think it might mean, then there is no possibility of a true meeting. Continue to open your mind. Open your mind in the center of that rigidity, that frozenness, that panic, and tell me what is discovered.

Nothing. I felt this frozenness and then nothing. But it's an alive nothing.
I feel free.

Excellent! Experience this nothingness without any name for it. Fall into the center of that. If there is any struggle, let it go. If there is any story line, put the story aside. Relax into this that you call nothing. See if it has any boundaries. See if you can make a separation between who you are and nothingness. If you are successful in making some separation between who you are and this nothingness, see if the separation exists in reality or only in the imagination.

• • •

I've had an experience like you were just talking about. I was in my bedroom one night and feeling uncomfortable. Something was wrong, and I'd spent a lifetime running away from what was uncomfortable. At a certain point I just saw it to be nothing, and then it was wonderful. After that I almost wished these bad feelings would come again.

Bad feelings and good feelings are all potential vehicles for sublime discovery. A secret is discovered in that instant of ceasing all activity designed to suppress, to cover, to deny, to run away from, to overcome, to follow, or to indulge. All activity of the mind ceases in the instant of direct experience.

This secret cannot be taught. It can only be discovered. There is no way to put this secret into words. All words fall short. What a surprise is discovered in the willingness, for just once, to stop all mental activity and *be*. It is the same with any discomfort or comfort—fear, boredom, frozenness, despair, bliss, or joy. The whole play of perceptions and emotions, whether uncomfortable or not, becomes a play that serves to deepen revelation of Self. Nothing has to be overcome, just met.

This is Self-inquiry, and Self-inquiry is endless. Limitless consciousness is present in all thoughts, all forms, all emotions, all experiences. Truth is present in everything, in all phenomena. That realization does not change. It only deepens in its changelessness. Experiences change. States change. Let them change. If there is an attempt to cling to a particular state, there is overlooking of what is present regardless of state.

Not wanting to experience, or wanting to keep a particular experience, creates the illusion of bondage. Until you are willing to experience anything, you will experience bondage because there will always be some mental activity generated around the desire to escape or the desire to indulge. If you are willing to experience anything, you discover that the experience of bondage is in fact illusion. The glue that holds this illusion together is the mental activity of escape or indulgence.

• • •

Direct experience is so simple that it is easily overlooked. In the course of any life-stream there have been many opportunities to face fear. There have been many times of repressing it or acting it out or being haunted by it. All of that activity feeds the belief that fear is a real entity. That it will swallow you, destroy you, drive you mad, or annihilate you is the story about fear.

I am telling you a profound yet simple truth. If you stop all mental running away or running toward, if you will be absolutely still, then direct experience *is*. In direct experience, you discover the emptiness of all phenomena. This emptiness is full, is impersonal consciousness, and is bliss. Mental activity is "thinking," what Papaji calls "chewing on bones from the graveyard." Stop chewing on these old bones searching for some nectar. Put these bones aside.

Fear may arise again. If it arises again, there is an even deeper opportunity. There may appear to be layer upon layer of negative emotion. Directly experiencing layer upon layer reveals illusions mentally carried forth since the beginning of time. Illusion discovered as illusion reveals Self.

In the instant of stopping and experiencing the emptiness in all phenomena for what it is, you discover the core of everything to be the Self. Self is all.

This is the greatest news. You are everywhere, in everything, waiting to be found, calling to be found. Let yourself be found.

Liberating Anger

Gangaji, when I see something that in my eyes isn't right, anger comes out spontaneously. In that moment, I feel I have to say something, and I feel good about that.

I have heard certain spiritual traditions say that anger is something that disturbs the mind and is a defilement. I don't understand this.

When anger is spoken about as a defilement or an obstruction, it is because bondage is experienced through the mental relationship with anger. Anger as an obsessive pattern of mind is an entanglement. Anger that is obstruction is anger that must either be obsessively expressed or obsessively denied. Then it is mind-generated and mind-perpetuated.

Natural anger is a great cyclone that washes clean. Natural, useful anger is the anger a mother feels when she sees something harmful happening to her child. Natural anger is not separate from compassion, and it is a great purifying force.

What must be examined is your relationship with anger. Is there some pattern of fearing it or of using it to avoid feeling hurt or sad or despairing? Anger must be met. This meeting naturally dissolves the protective relationship, and then you will see you needn't act as a slave to anger.

Many religious teachings are given as codes of conduct. Hearing that anger is an obstruction gets interpreted as instruction to suppress anger. Habitual suppression only turns anger into numbness or rigidity. The goal of true spirituality is freedom. In freedom there is power, softness, and welcoming, so that even the demon anger is liberated. When anger is liberated, it serves the truth. When it is bound by personal identification, it serves the ego.

Look into the deepest meaning of teachings. Teachings are first given to allow people to gather in the same enclosed space together. You must have noticed that humans are a very strange species. We are both social and anti-social. Both polarities are very strong. There is a great amount of love possible and a great amount of hate possible. If you get four or more people in a room together for any length of time, and there is just wildness of expression, horrible problems are created.

There is a certain level of socialization that allows people to come together. There is no error in this, and it is not a mistake to take on certain conditioning that allows you to put your animal instincts aside. If you look into the animal kingdom, there is no animal quite as ferocious as the human animal. It has nearly conquered the planet.

There is a kind of spiritual or religious conditioning that allows people to come together so that they can hear the news of this precious treasure. As you leave your shoes outside the door, you leave your normal mode of expression outside the door, so that perhaps you can receive what is being offered. If you stop with this level of understanding, then leaving shoes outside the door becomes a practice, and you are always leaving your shoes somewhere, or always repressing some emotion as if that is where the truth lies. This kind of conditioning is only a means, so don't get stuck in the means. There is the possibility of hearing what is deeper than either repression or expression.

Considerations about anger are particularly tricky because anger does not facilitate harmony in groups or family gatherings. There can be no harmony if everybody is always expressing their anger. Always repressing anger does not work either. It makes society work better as a machine, and it allows people to gather, but the gathering is sterile and bound by the law of repression. It is possible to meet anger directly and discover what is at the core of anger. In this meeting, you can recognize true harmony, which is the core of your true nature, deeper than your human animal nature.

I do not mean to meet anger in analysis, although that may be appropriate at a certain stage. I am speaking about simply meeting anger—not denying it, not expressing it, but simply meeting it. In a true meeting, you discover what all teachings have promised. You discover that there is nothing separate from God. There is nothing excluded from the Absolute. Your physical body is not excluded from that. Your mind-stream is not excluded from that. Your emotional body is not excluded from that. With this realization, you can begin to hear God speak itself in all forms.

Meet anger now. Then your life is in service to that which is revealed in that meeting. Your whole life is realized to be an expression of Self meeting Itself. Then whatever mood or weather pattern appears, it is in service to truth quite miraculously and mysteriously.

• • •

The other night when I came to satsang I was experiencing a lot of rage. I hadn't been acting it out, but I still got caught in the idea that I had to do something about it, so it became more and more of a congestion.

When you experienced the rage and the congestion and the sense that you had to do something with it, was there a shift?

The shift was in sitting here and being reminded that I am not the rage or the issues. Previously I had gotten to the point where I felt that I had to resolve the rage before I could be free of it. Being here in satsang, I was able to have the rage, and yet I didn't feel that pressure to give up the rage to be free.

You didn't have to repress it, and you didn't have to act it out. You did not have to do anything with it.

Right.

Because you realized it was not the determinant of who you are?

True. What I was realizing today is that the emotional being also needs tending, just like we have to clean the house and tend to our body.

How did you discover to best tend the emotional body?

By not identifying with it.

Excellent. This is emotional liberation. *You* are already free. Now you are speaking of liberating ideas and concepts, whether they are in the physical body, the emotional body, or the mental body. You directly discovered liberating the impulse to do something with rage by not touching any story around it. Then naturally, as you say, rage is free to move, free to finish, free to resolve itself. It does not need picking and dissecting.

By realizing who you are, everything is tended. The world is tended. I do not mean tended so that you can drift into complacency where you once again ignore or deny emotions that arise. Realization is in the present. It is not something in the past. If you relegate it to the past and then rage arises, the same pattern will reincarnate.

In every moment you have the absolute freedom to discover yourself to be freedom. In that discovery, everything is tended. Then the mind is a conduit for revelation. Insights around rage and hurt and fear will arise naturally.

What did you mean when you said not touching any story?

I mean not to grasp for a story line that justifies the emotion and not to reject with a story line that condemns the emotion. Without grasping or rejecting, there is no work for the ego. When rage arose in you, there was a tendency to want to do something with it. Even if that meant to just sit on it or endure it. If you are willing for rage to arise, and you neither do anything to drive it away nor to act it out, neither repress it nor express it, then you will see in an instant what is deeper—whether you see a deeper emotion or whether you see into the depth of being.

It's real trickery.

Expose the trickery of the mind. The mind can be very subtle. The challenge is in being attentive to this very subtle tendency to move into mental activity. For instance, if the emotion arising had been bliss, the tendency might have been to try and keep it. Attempting to keep bliss doesn't work of course. If you simply let bliss be, with no story line attached to it, the great good news is that bliss dissolves into deeper bliss which finally is beyond definition.

This is the good news about both negative and positive emotions. The negative emotions are limited. Their lifetime is based on past mental relationships. Whether it is your mother's past mental relationships or your own or society's, past patterns of relating to negative emotions cause present and future patterns of relationship to arise. The true emotions of bliss and joy are causeless and limitless.

This is extraordinary news! If you are willing neither to grasp nor reject bliss, and you are willing neither to grasp nor reject rage, you will discover the limitlessness of your true nature as joyous and blissful. In the moment of willingness, as the history is dropped, the emotion is finished, and you are headed in the direction of the experience of the truth of your being.

Dropping the story exposes the trickery. It is a trick we have played on ourselves for a long, long time. Be willing to finish the trick.

Can I go a step further?

Oh yes, please.

I have the tendency to make an effort to be present.

In the moment of being aware of efforting *to be*, relax. The investment in efforting is only perpetuated by following thoughts of rejecting or grasping, and you know these thoughts very well. They are not fresh, original thoughts. These old, worn thoughts are not insights and revelations. You know them by the sense in your body. You know them by the contraction or the sanctimoniousness that follows these thoughts. You know the story line very well, so don't touch it. If you do not touch it, these thoughts cannot continue. It is so simple.

It is very challenging.

Simplicity is only challenging because we are conditioned to effort and work and do and achieve. In the spiritual search what we are working at and doing and achieving is to arrive where we already are! You have experienced this simplicity. It is always present in its limitless vastness. It is already here in the joy of itself, in the peace of itself, in the perfection of itself.

The exposure of the trickery is simply the exposure of the apparent veil caused by following thoughts like, "I have to do something with rage."

Then before I know it, I'm in the game again.

Yes, but now you know how to play the game. So play it well. Play it deeply. Play it ruthlessly, honestly, effortlessly. Real playing is vigilance. When it is effortless, it plays itself.

Let the challenges come! They are exhilarating! You will be thrown on the mat, and thrown on the mat, and thrown on the mat. Pretty soon you will cease taking the emotion personally. You will stop the mind activity.

I am not speaking of withdrawal from life, or of going into a dissociated state, or of stopping the play. Play fully. To play fully, stop your personal identification. Stop imagining that you are a particular player. You are in totality the player, the played, and the play itself.

To make my life vigilance means to give up my process of thought and counter thought. What a challenge. Effortless being is the simplest yet the deepest challenge of a lifetime. I am ready. Thank you.

• • •

I have found that despair which anger covers. Are you saying that I should just feel the despair?

Stop running from it. Dive into the core of it. You know you have not surrendered when despair lasts in duration. You may spend a night in despair, or a day in despair, but the moment the struggle against despair stops, where is despair? It is the struggle with despair or the acting out of despair that gives despair its life. It is your imagination that keeps the struggle going.

Mental wards are filled with people who are struggling against emotions by either suppression or dramatization of these emotions. The psychotic experience is of fragmentation, which is very different from dissolution. In psychosis, the ego is experienced as being fragmented into multiple parts. I am not recommending fragmentation! I am speaking about the possibility of the dissolution of the false *I*. Ego means false *I*.

At the gate of despair, despair appears endless, and all neurotic impulses arise to avoid being consumed by it. The psychotic impulse is to act out despair in some way, such as suicide.

Is the despair limitless?

The revelatory discovery is that the despair is, at most, limited. If you dive into the core of despair, you discover no despair at all. What *is* limitless is peace, silence, joy. If you dive into peace, it doesn't dissolve. Isn't that amazing? Peace does not dissolve. Your idea of who you are dissolves, and you are revealed as peace. You are silence, you are joy, and you are fathomless, endless, limitless.

It is no good though just to hear me say it. This is something you must directly experience.

• • •

I can meet the sadness about the anger, especially sitting here with you, but in meeting anger itself, I feel like a mouse meeting a tiger.

Yes, and the impulse arises to take some kind of action to defend the mouse, or to run into your little hole and hide. I am suggesting that you do not hide from anger. Do not take some kind of stance with anger, either by expressing it or by discharging it. Then the true nature of anger is revealed.

I do not have anything against anger. I am not saying you should live your life never expressing anger, never shouting. What kind of life is that? Anger can be quite beautiful unless it is the guard dog that keeps you from experiencing patterns of hurt or fear or the basic vulnerability of being human.

Usually, there is some kind of relationship with anger that presupposes anger to be a force that will devour you. Be willing, in immovability, to be devoured by this fire. Willingness to be devoured means that you are not ignoring it, not using it for some egocentric purpose, and not trying to get rid of it.

I let the anger happen when it happens, but I still don't get it. I remember you said, "Stop, just stop." Well, if I try to do that, it gets much, much worse.

Do you mean you are seeing the storehouse of anger you have been sitting on? If so, good. You are seeing it more deeply than some easily justifiable response. This is what is supposed to happen.

It feels like I am going to explode, and that explosion is such a physical experience. You were speaking the other day of the possibility of some things being in our genes, in our DNA. That's just what it feels like. My father got angry in exactly the same way.

I am not speaking about *getting* angry. I am not speaking about something needing to be done with the anger. I am speaking about directly experiencing anger. For direct experience, you cannot *get* angry. Getting angry indicates that you still have some story about the anger, either that it should be there or that it should not be there. If you think that anger should not be there, you expend energy trying to get rid of it. If you think that anger should be there, you expend energy trying to express it and justify it.

I am speaking of being devoured by being still. Stillness penetrates into the core of the anger attack. In this moment of stillness, in the eye of the emotional hurricane, you stop the anger karma of your form, and your father's form, and all that has been passed on to you and accumulated and believed to be real.

Surrender. Be crucified on the cross of anger. To be crucified, you cannot move. You are tied up, so you cannot lash out at anyone, not even yourself. You are in a very awkward position, so you cannot go to sleep or ignore the anger. You cannot pretend that it is not happening. You can make no move to deal with the idea that anger is so big it will explode you.

For some people there is fear of the anger itself. For others it may be fear of insanity, of going berserk. Ironically, out of following the fear that one might go berserk, one usually expresses anger in either covertly or overtly insane ways. People who are in psychotic wards are either desperately attempting not to go berserk or are caught in the grip of what gets called "expression."

There is a certain point when you say, as the Buddha said, "I will not be moved. If I explode, so be it. If this is the end of my form through some kind of spontaneous combustion, so be it. If all the negative forces of my whole lineage come in and tear me apart, so be it." In immovability, you will see the truth of anger, and you will be able to give up the old destructive game. Getting off the wheel of samsara means to give up the game. Giving up the game is possible by being willing to meet whatever arises without moving.

In the midst of anger, I can't feel that which does not move. Although I feel it sitting here with you, I can't say that the quiet is available for me when I'm angry.

Then you are not in the center of the anger. You are attending to the periphery by maintaining some story about the anger. In the maintenance of the story, all you can relate to is the story. The story is held together by mental activity. Drop the story. It takes some degree of effort to continue the story. Give up being right. Give up being wrong. Give up being the victim. Give up being the aggressor. Give up everything your parents did to you, your lover did to you, and the world did to you. Give up everything you did to your parents, you did to your lover, and you did to the world. Give it all up. Give up the world.

This is not a usual or normal moment! What is normal is to be in a kind of functioning neurosis of sometimes controlling the anger, sometimes repressing the anger, sometimes discharging the anger, sometimes expressing the anger.

I am not saying that any of these mental activities are wrong. There is a time and place for them all. I am saying that an undiscovered treasure remains undiscovered by imagining that these strategies are the limit of what is available in the moment of anger arising. The only way possible to penetrate to the core of anger is to leave behind every idea about anger. To penetrate to the core of any phenomenon you must give up every idea about that phenomenon and the one who is penetrating.

To penetrate the ocean, to penetrate the sunset, to penetrate what is called love, to penetrate anything, you have to release your world of concepts. Before penetration, there is a story about an experience or about a phenomenon. In this case we are speaking of anger. Anger can have enormous charge to it. There can be an enormous investment in the story which holds the charge together. Maybe it is a genetic story. Maybe it does not even have words to it.

With anger comes the impulse to move. It is a powerful, physical instinct, but what is deeper and more powerful than any instinct? This is what must be discovered for there to be lasting happiness.

What must be cut is the identification that the anger is more powerful than that which it arises in. You are that in which all phenomena arise. When you discover you are that, phenomena are just phenomena, and you realize whatever their display, they are limited in duration and power.

Discover what has always been. Before that discovery your attention is fixated on your personal life, its personal anger, and its personal joys. There is no need to settle for that. There is the vast sky of Being that is inviting you to meet it. In order to enter, turn your attention away from this one little wisp of cloud called "Me and my anger." In order to shift your attention away from that, penetrate through it to the source. Penetrate to the beginning, not to the initial event of anger but to the source of all events, all display, all emotions.

If you play in the waves of the ocean, you know that in order to penetrate into the ocean, sometimes you must move through the waves. The waves are very close to the shore, so you must dive right through them, rather than continuing to run away because you imagine they have the power to keep you out of the depths of the ocean. You want to penetrate into the ocean, but big waves keep chasing you out of the ocean onto the shore. If you see someone who is in the depths of the ocean, you may ask, "How did you get there?"

"Through the wave!"

"But I can't. It may destroy me."

"Just dive right through and see."

Be willing to be swallowed by the ocean of Being. Face the fear of destruction. Of course the bigger the wave, the deeper you must dive. The more you dive, the deeper you can dive and the less power the waves have in your life. In this willingness, the egocentric activity of mind has no power. A life truly lived is not fixated on preservation. In fact, the prayer is that everything that *can* be destroyed be revealed *as* destroyed. This is Shiva's message to you. This is the Guru's gift. In one instant everything is wiped out, everything is destroyed. Then what is beyond destruction is Self-apparent.

I am not saying willingness is usual or known or easy to do. It is beyond easy or difficult to do. It is impossible to do. Willingness is the absolute ease present when you do not "do." Our training is to do something, and that is where your trouble is. You want to figure out how to do it. If you can figure out how to do it, then when it comes up and bothers you again, you know how to get rid of it.

This is no good! You have to first discover what *it* is. When you discover that the wave is, in fact, never separate from the ocean, why do you need to get rid of it? When you no longer have to get rid of anger, it is not as you have previously experienced it. It is not as you have believed it to be. The world is not as you have known it to be. You are not as you have known yourself to be.

I can see already you sense the relief. Realization cannot be done. If you *really* hear this, that realization cannot be done, then you will stop trying to do anything to be realized. What a relief! Realization is not about learning some task. Tasks can be learned and done. Lessons can be learned, languages can be learned, skills can be learned. Freedom is not a skill to be learned. You cannot learn who you are. You cannot do who you are. You cannot practice who you are. It is impossible. You can only be who you are.

I still want to ask you and Papaji and Ramana for help with the anger.

You are surrounded by help. You do not even need to ask anymore. Just check and see if it is there. You have asked deeply, truly, with your whole heart, and help has been promised. Now check. Rather than asking for more help, receive the help that is waiting for you.

I feel luckier than the person who has everything this world could offer, because I have what the world doesn't offer!

This is the secret of recognizing what is already given. In this instant, where is all the suffering? You will see that this very anger that you were afraid of revealed that help. Then anger, despair, insanity, whatever the demon may be, reveals the limitless help that you have asked for and is eternally given. How could it not be so? You are only asking your Self. When you check, you are overcome with gratitude. What luck!

Of course, anger may be attracted to that luck. Luck is a bright light shining in the midst of a dark forest. All kinds of creatures may come to see what is going on. Do you know that the rhinoceros charges fires in the forest? Let the rhinoceros come in. Then perhaps the rhinoceros will discover what is at the core of its charging. What a discovery! Then the rhinoceros is liberated, anger is liberated, and so much more.

I can speak about these things, but I cannot speak about what is more. The capacity has not been formed in the brain to speak about that. That is the truth of who you are.

• • •

The anger I feel is a very rajasic* energy.

Like a volcano erupting?

Yes, like that.

Don't take it personally.

Okay! (laughing) Say more.

To not take it personally means to unmovingly discover what is at the core. Then you will discover what is deeper than the anger. Then the anger will just be an energy, a voltage around the core.

I feel like that energy drives me. Sometimes I don't know what to do with that energy.

Yes, a volcano is large. An eruption of that volcano is huge, and it can cause much destruction.

Don't do anything to let anger come, and don't do anything to repress it. Then this rajasic energy is an ally, a wind horse, a gift. It is the gift of the lightening bolt when you realize what is absolutely untouched, unmoved, and undisturbed. It reveals the truth of what is indestructible.

As long as anger is being repressed or as long as anger is being acted out, indestructibleness is being overlooked. That indestructibleness is your true Self.

Do you follow this?

rajasic* - Fiery, active.

Yes, but it's still hard to let it in.

What will be lost if you let it in?

Safety.

Yes! That's right. Very accurate answer. Somehow anger has been used for protection, hasn't it?

Yes, maybe.

Well, you said safety would be lost, so if you let this in, then you don't have the anger as a controlling force.

In this moment, why not just experience total lack of safety.

Okay.

Really? Are you sure you're not holding on to some possibility of safety? I am speaking of a *total* lack of safety.

It's actually exhilarating to stand up here and speak to you with no protection.

That's right. You are speaking of vulnerability. Vulnerability is actually exhilarating, isn't it? That which is feared—vulnerability, lack of safety—when experienced, is actually quite wonderful.

As long as you are falsely identified as the body, vulnerability will be fought. The body must be protected, must be fed, must be clothed, and must be sheltered, or it will be destroyed. As you know, the body will eventually be destroyed anyway, so there is no real safety for the body.

In the moment you are truly willing to experience no safety anywhere, identification is cut, and you recognize what *is* indestructible. Not the body, the body is obviously destructible. What animates the body, what the body exists in, is Life, and Life is indestructible. Not the particular life-form, but Life which gives the life-form its Life. Life is awareness, intelligence, love. This is who you are. In your willingness to experience vulnerability, to experience lack of safety, to experience the fear that is under the impulse to erupt, there is the potential to realize yourself as that indestructibility. Then your rajasic nature will be a servant to that. Then you will roar, and the roar of awakening is a roar of welcome.

States and Experiences

Omnipresent Being, revealed in the most extraordinary events and the most ordinary events, is the sublime realization of truth. The most sublime state follows the revelation of eternal presence. To be true to that revelation—whether you have experienced it in a split second, or an hour, or a week, or a year, or thirty years—is to honor and serve it all the days of your lifetime.

• • •

I know that my state of consciousness, in this moment, is perfect, is God, but I also feel I've experienced states that seemed more like God.

So what? A mountain can seem more perfect than a cockroach. That is the nature of seeming. That is the nature of comparison. In truth, they are the same perfection. If you are really to receive that which seems more like God—some mountain of power—and you receive it all the way, then you will recognize that here too, in this ordinary state, is the same God. Then there is no longer any suffering based on comparison of states.

As awesome and beautiful as special states are, they are still states. Of course, they are wonderful, but to honor these special states, to honor the mountain, to honor the guru, go all the way. You will see that *all the way* is stateless and is present *all ways*. Then you cannot create suffering over wanting to feel some other particular, special state. Do you understand that the desire for a particular state is a trap of the mind?

If you attempt to hold some special state together, or to find it again, or to recreate it in the future, you begin to deny what is simply here in all ways, and the cycle of suffering is perpetuated.

Does effort to bring a special state back work?

Well, no, it hasn't.

In your attempt to try to recreate some special state, you are basing what you want on what you had in the past. In this attempt, you overlook what you have now. This that you have now is not past, not future, and not even present. It is timeless. What is timeless is Self, God, Perfection. Anything not here in all ways simply appears to be here and then disappears from here.

There are many teachers who can work magic to evoke certain states. That is very useful if the magical state points to that which is stateless. If it does not, then it is just another magic trip. Being hooked into following magic does not reveal fulfillment. You know that with the biggest highs come the lowest lows. That is the nature of manifestation. I am not saying don't let the biggest highs come. Let them come. The biggest highs, the lowest lows, let them come. What remains through the highs and through the lows? This is essential. What is untouched by both the lowest low and the highest high? The highest high reflects eternal, stateless truth, which is also present in the lowest low! Recognize that peace and truth can be revealed in any state.

Just for one split second, be who you are. If you are in love with that, then let it overflow. Stop trying to hide it, control it, contain it, fix it, do it, or recreate it. Just let it overflow.

Does this bring satisfaction?

I guess so. I guess I'm there now. This must be it.

Not if it is just a guess. That is the mind's trick. Doubtless conviction is the natural result of realization. Not a guess, not a hope, not a thought.

This moment is It. But realizing it is very different from guessing it, hoping it, thinking it, or even experiencing it.

Realizing it is different from experiencing it?

Yes, yes, yes! Experience comes and goes; realization does not move.

The beings that I have the most respect for speak as if the ego sense of being a separate I completely disappears.

Yes, and that realization is recognized as the eternal purity before, during, and after all states.

In timelessness, there is no experience, no experiencer. There is just pure consciousness, free of any illusion of form and name. From that, there is an unforeseeable state of bliss and ecstasy where one can experience, *I am one with everything, I am Perfection, I am God, I am Self.*

This that is permanent is revealed in realization, and is the realization. It is exactly the same in *individual* and in *all*. It does not move. Perfection is present whether you always realize yourself to be one with perfection or whether you experience yourself as separate from perfection. Perfection does not move. Your mind appears to move in this perfection.

In that highest state you refer to, there is no possibility of thinking yourself separate. Now, if you think yourself separate again and a "lower" state comes, find out what has changed and what has not changed. That is all. It is that simple. Do you think God only wears glowing robes? Do you think God is clothed? God is only clothed by your mind.

• • •

Some months ago, after being exposed to this understanding and to your teachings, I experienced a settling in. I physiologically settled down and got quiet. It came by itself. There was nothing that I did for it.

When you stop doing, there is a natural resting.

It is very important to understand this. You are absolutely

correct in that it was nothing that you did, but you must also see the other side of that.

I don't think I see the other side.

What were you doing that kept you from what you call "experience of settling"?

Wondering what the experience was about.

Wondering is mental doing.

I was looking for it, desiring it.

This is all mental doing. Do you see? When there is penetration by truth, doing stops, and revelation is apparent.

It seemed to start with a glimpse of what reality is, and it seemed to be a little shimmering, transparent something or other out of the corner of my eye. Then the sinking in happened. Then good experiences came and went on their own, and with them came the understanding that this is all grace; there is nothing I can do for this.

You are speaking accurately. Mysteriously, the embrace of grace has chosen you. Out of all the people who perhaps worked harder, did better things, gave more, sacrificed more, somehow, as you say, you are graced with this divine welcoming.

You can spend time resisting grace, denying grace, and feeling unworthy of grace, or you can simply give your life totally to grace, to be enfolded in this embrace.

For months this went on, and it felt completely natural. The one thing that seemed to be missing was that I still felt like myself having these experiences. I didn't feel like "nothing" having these experiences, and I wonder about that.

What do you mean when you say "myself"? Who was, and is, having these experiences?

It felt as if it was the personality.

Can a personality have experiences? Is there any inherent animation of personality?

No. Without the spirit, it's nothing.

When you dissect personality, it is primarily gestures—emotional gestures, physical gestures, mental gestures.

And habits.

Can habits experience anything?

You are at the crux of the dilemma. You identify yourself as personality, until you actually see that personality is nothing but habits. When you look at habits and dissect them even closer, you will see they are nothing but gestures.

What is a gesture? Who owns a gesture? Personality, habit, and gesture are all inert. It's as if you are saying what a wonderful day your dress had yesterday.

You said you still felt like yourself. I am saying that you are no *thing*. You are not a personality, even though you wear a personality. Perhaps you wear it so tightly that you have overlooked that if you drop it, you remain whole and full, while it lies lifeless on the floor. The mistake is objectifying yourself and assigning that objectification to a body, a personality, or an emotional state. You are the awareness of all—all states, all bodies, all personalities, all everything, all nothing. Awareness is not a *thing*.

That was my next question. One time during this delight-ful period of my life, I woke up at night for no apparent reason and decided while I'm awake, why not inquire, "Who am I?" Unlike the other times when I had inquired, this time I immediately experienced who I was. What I saw was a com-plete emptiness, a complete nothingness.

Who saw this?

(laughing) That's a good question.

That laughter is a good answer.

Who saw this? (laughing)
Is that it!!!? I can see that it's not a thing!

Yes! Very good. You are not a thing. Are you nothing?

Nothing and not nothing!

Yes! Yes! This is very important because often there is an experience of nothingness, and then because that experience is in memory somewhere, nothingness then becomes a some-thingness named nothingness.

Then I had a sled riding accident and hit my tailbone very hard. It seemed as if instantly a switch was flipped. Everything I had known, the silence that was everywhere, that was me, the cosmic truth that I seem to intuit now, just stopped.

So you were pulled back into physical incarnation.

My teacher picked me up and tossed me across the sea, back into my past life. He said, "Now, from there, you tell me, who are you?"

At first I thought, *Oh, how I long to go back to the samadhi* of being at the feet of my beloved Master.*

And he said, "Don't come here. You have discovered it here; now discover it there."

Do you think that who you are is limited to some experience of bliss? Do you think that who you are disappears when the nervous system impulse of cosmic consciousness shifts to the nervous system impulse of mundane consciousness?

What has remained? What has been constant throughout all shifts?

---

* samadhi - Rapturous absorption in bliss.

Now, *you* tell *me*, who are you?

There is something that has remained. It just seems less available.

Really? Where are you looking for it?

That's my confusion.

Then I suspect you are looking toward some imagery or some memory or some desire for sensual or intellectual stimulation.

Look to the looker and tell me, what happens to the concept of availability?

Well, here now, availability is irrelevant.

That's right. It does not make any sense. Who is there left to measure? Who measures in the first place, and by what indicator?

I see that measurement is only in the mind.

Yes, you were making a boundary between more and less. You believed the boundary between the experience of more and the experience of less to be real. What is the reality of that boundary?

From the experience of being in a body, from the experience of being a person, of having had revealed to you the limitlessness, the no-thingness of who one truly is, now, from

123

this experience, tell me what is excluded from cosmic consciousness? What is excluded from the truth of who one is?

Nothing. All is included.

I am happy that you had this whack to the base of your spine. Otherwise, you might have been preaching transcendentalism. The experience and the realization of transcendentalism is exquisite and crucial, yet the circle must be completed.

I remember Papaji said to me, "So now, speak to me from the unspeakable place. Speak to me!"

I said, "Papaji, it is impossible to speak from that place."

Then I would drift into an experience of samadhi, and he would again say, "Now! Now! Now! Come! Speak! Right now!"

Again I said, "Papaji, I can't speak from that place."

Finally he said, "Then come back and speak. Come back and speak."

Now from coming back, tell me, where were you, and where can you go from here?

There is only here.

Yes. See only here.

• • •

"Here" has different flavors at different times?

Here has no flavor whatsoever, yet different flavors pass through.

Clear light, when refracted, reveals a rainbow, yet as clear light, there are no colors. If you get attached to the rainbow, you overlook the realization of clear light—clear of color, clear of name, clear of form. If you realize clear light, then when name and form appear, they are more proof of clear light. Name and form are not obstacles to pure awareness. Name and form are refractions of pure awareness.

We have spent lifetimes clinging to some idea of name and form, and then in a very lucky lifetime, there is penetration by this unspeakable, mysterious, divine grace which reveals in an instant the vast emptiness of one's true nature.

Why is there clinging?

You must like to cling because you have spent so much time clinging. Now you have the opportunity also to experience the feeling of release.

You like experiencing your Self in all ways. I am not saying clinging is wrong. However, if you believe it to be necessary for the revelation of who you are, you are simply mistaken. Life does not need to cling to life to be life.

You hide because you like to be found. You experience separation because you love the experience of reunion. You experience being lost in the woods, so that you can experience the relief of finding your way home. All of this occurs *here* where you always already are.

There is nothing wrong with experience. This is the play of God, the play of Perfection. If you are ready to be found, be still. If you are not ready, continue your experience of being lost and suffering. When you are ready, you will know it. You will raise your hand, and you will say, "I have a passion for truth even greater than my likes of wanderings. I have a love of truth even greater than any other infatuations."

You will see truth is here, waiting, whatever flavors, experiences, or states are passing through.

• • •

Recently, I had an experience of sitting on the beach, and I felt myself go far out. At that point, I really knew that there was no individual I. It was an amazing experience of pure intelligence. Then there was a moment when I remembered my name and came back into my known self.

Yes?

And yet, I did not have in that experience the feeling of love that I have felt at other times, in other experiences. Part of me was surprised, thinking, "I am experiencing universal intelligence, but I am not experiencing love, so I had better get back in my body."

When you speak of this experience, you are speaking of a moment out of time where Self recognizes Itself as pure, vast intelligence. The fear that love was missing comes from a past mistake. The mistake is some prior definition of love believed to be the reality of love.

The body is the conduit for the sensual experience of love

as love is defined. You are speaking of having experienced phenomena through the sensory nervous system and then having concluded that certain sensations prove or disprove love. Usually the conclusion is that love has warmth or tingling or any number of sensations—some pleasant, some unpleasant—as its components. No particular sensations, therefore, means no love.

What follows is a fear that if we experience pure consciousness or nothingness, then we might lose our experience of love or compassion.

There is a point where the concept of love, as it has been defined, is lost. A point when there is only pure intelligence.

If you accept pure intelligence with no holding back for some idea of love, you will see that love is revealed in more subtle ways than any one feeling or group of sensations can claim.

Once one has had such an experience, once one has had a glimpse of who one really is, then how does that experience become the permanent reality of one's life?

Until one has had some glimpse, all talk of Perfection, of Truth or God is abstract and theoretical—a hope or a belief or a write-off. Once there has been a glimpse, then we can speak of choice, of what is to be honored, of what is to be surrendered to in the face of all seeming proof to the contrary. After this glimpse, there is really free choice, regardless of the tidal wave of conditioned existence that may arise or the aeons of practiced denial that may come to attack.

Your question is how to make this sublime experience a permanent reality. Honor, serve, and surrender to That which is revealed. Regardless of what you are feeling, regardless of circumstance, regardless of state of mind, regardless of mental evaluation . . . just surrender to That.

This surrender, once again, is the transmission that comes from Ramana as *Be Still*. In stillness, That which is glimpsed is revealed to be That which is permanent, to be That who one is.

This sacred choice takes enormous resolve—enormous, unrelenting, effortless resolve. Effortless resolve is the secret, because if resolve requires effort, it is something that must be maintained and practiced. This resolve needs to be so huge that it is present twenty-four hours a day, every instant. Whenever an inkling of some propensity to identify oneself as the sufferer arises, this resolve must be present. It must be present night and day, sleeping, waking, eating, moving, being happy, being sad, feeling high, and feeling low. Resolve is the effortless attention to what is effortlessly present at every instant.

● ● ●

A few mornings ago I meditated on, "Who am I?" I am going to try and describe this, even though I know it is not accurate. What I experienced and the reason it's not accurate, is that there was no "I." The "I" disappeared.

This is accurate!

It was consciousness aware of consciousness as consciousness.

Oh, this is beautiful!

And it was so blissful.

Yes, it is! It *is* blissful.

I felt like I was exploding.

Don't even say *was*. Don't put realization in the past tense. It *is*. The explosion is the byproduct of the realization of consciousness conscious of Itself. Not as some separate *I*, but as Itself in Its totality. Yes, bliss is the nature of that discovery. Expansion is the nature of that discovery. Originality is the nature of that discovery. That which has never been thought is the nature of that discovery.

Now the experience has left me, and it makes me wonder if there was any realization at all.

There is a slight but essential misunderstanding here.

The experience of the bliss of that explosion is still an experience, and all experience is limited. Before that experience occurred, it wasn't. There is a time when experience occurs, and there is a time when experience is gone.

In true recognition, there is the recognition of what simply *is*. The explosion is the byproduct of that recognition. You turned your attention away from the source of the explosion, and you began to cling to the byproduct as the indication that now you are some place, now you are enlightened, now you are fulfilled.

In the opening that follows this divine explosion, anything that has been suppressed is likely to arise. If there is no clinging to the bliss that has been experienced, you will have no more need for any particular experience and will recognize, finally, all experiences reveal That.

What I am pointing to is deeper than any particular state or experience. Realization does not contradict human experience. This human wave occurs in consciousness, as consciousness in the form of wave of consciousness. Conscious recognition of Itself does not need the flattening of the wave. Wave appears as wave as long as it appears as wave. As long as there is experiencing, there is also human experience.

There will be, and are, sublime, unforeseeable experiences of ecstasy, peace, and clarity, but these are still not *It*. The *It* is realization fresh in every moment: *I am This! I am This that is speaking. I am This that is listening. I am this That is spoken. I am beyond all that is spoken and heard and present in all that is spoken and heard.*

● ● ●

Why am I so happy all the time and I'm still not satisfied?

You are paying attention to the experience and not to the awareness of the experience. Bliss and happiness are states. As states, they are still illusion, and ultimately you are never satisfied with illusion.

I realize that in order to stop identifying myself with the illusion, it takes trust. Also, deference to a higher Self, which is something that I may not always be able to sustain the awareness of.

You are still speaking of some object or some particular state. You say, "I want to sustain the awareness of ecstasy," or, "I want to sustain the awareness of clarity," or, "I want to sustain the awareness of higher Self." These are all states. They are beautiful states, but they are only states, and as states, they come and they go. The awareness of these states needs no sustaining. Awareness is Self-sustaining.

Most of the great spiritual traditions speak of establishment and sustaining. Really what is being pointed to is that which is already, firmly, wholly established as that. That which is already Self-sustained. That which is already Self-evident. If you begin the effort of trying to sustain something, then again there is a split in the mind. You think, *I must sustain this, because this is who I really am.* If this is who you really are, then this *is* who you *really* are, *period.* You are not separate from who you are with the need or the option to either sustain yourself or lose yourself.

The challenge is total trust because the entrancement is that you are not That. You believe you are some image of yourself, or some physical representation, or some sensation, and with this belief comes fear. With fear, mental scurrying and searching begin for what is perceived to be lost. At some moment of grace, there is the revelation of trust. Relax into that trust, and let it be done.

There may be some very intense moments. There may be experiences of shaking and terror and suffering. These moments pass. What is left is clarity itself. If you search for clarity and wisdom, you overlook that the searcher itself is part of the illusion. The idea of a lower self and a higher self is the illusion. There is only the Self, sometimes dressed in rags, sometimes dressed in royal robes. Throw your rags away. Because you have worn these rags for aeons, you have infused them with a reality that is illusory.

Recognize that your old rags are nothing. They are just concepts that are disintegrating as we speak. Your body is disintegrating as we speak. Your world is disintegrating as we speak.

What remains? What is the power that gives life to everything? Rags, robes, bodies, worlds? Discover this. This that has given power to "higher self" is Self, period. It is who you are.

When your rags are long gone, when your body is long gone, Self remains. Discover this even while wearing your body, and you will discover great happiness, great peace, great joy, and beyond.

Don't wear old rags or royal robes. Be naked in the splendor of the truth of who you are.

• • •

I've made the feeling of bliss I experience in my heart a prerequisite for freedom, and I feel like it's a burden.

Be willing to give up all burdens including feelings of bliss. Clinging to bliss is where many people get hooked. You can see that if you attempt to cling to feelings of bliss, and then there is no bliss, there is great and unnecessary suffering. If you are willing to release everything, then the bliss behind the bliss that does not need to be blissful to be bliss is revealed— the dance behind the dancing that does not need movement for its dance; the music behind the music; the core.

• • •

What about the experience of pain in our bodies?

If you identify that you are the experience of pain, and then attempt to reject the pain, there is unnecessary suffering.

Regardless of whatever experience there is, whether it be of pain, or of joy, or of no sensory experience, there is always pure awareness present. Awareness is not bound by any name or experience. Your true name is that namelessness. Claim it. It belongs to you.

And when there is awareness of pleasure?

Pleasure is a sensory experience. It comes and it goes. If you chase pleasure, you end up with unnecessary suffering.

Pain is a sensory experience. It comes and goes. If you reject pain, you end up with unnecessary suffering.

Drop everything, including and most essentially the image or the thought of the one who is chasing the pleasure, and the one who is running from the pain.

Rather than focusing on the experience of pleasure or the experience of pain, find the experiencer, and see if that is limited. See if both pain and pleasure, as well as all other states, begin and end there. See if that has any needs, any aversions, any boundaries.

• • •

I find I desire pleasure.

Who desires pleasure?

You have assumed you are a thing, somebody, but this is a false assumption. When you actually return to *I*, what is pleasure and pain in that?

Don't move from *I*. You say, "*I* desire pleasure." Erase pleasure, erase desire, and now, just *I*.

Stay right there, and speak from That.

I can't find who "I" is.

But when you look for *I*, who is found?

Nothing.

Is this nothing a dead, blank nothing, or is this nothing limitlessness itself?

I think so.

You think so? You must know so. This is why you are

here. It is time to stop thinking about it! It is confidence in who you are that you are seeking, isn't it? Conviction, not some idea that *I* is limitless, but the direct experience.

You say, "I can't find anything there," and this is the truth.

Now, tell me, what *is* there? Is awareness there?

Yes.

You can find no *thing*, just awareness? Excellent! Remain in the awareness of awareness—not awareness as some *thing* or some *body*, just pure awareness. In your willingness to more deeply experience awareness, everything you have been searching for in some *thing* is revealed. Awareness is the source of all revelation.

This that is glimpsed in that instant is the invitation. Come Home. Return to what has always been.

Return to the simplicity of *I* itself. Not simplicity that is limited or conceptual, but the immeasurable simplicity of *I*. Then revelations happen naturally, without any searching or calibrating or measuring. This is the promise.

• • •

I made a discovery since the last time I talked with you. I was experiencing ecstasy, and I believe that this was a form of the mind's resistance to going deeper. When I vowed to just be, the excitement wasn't there.

The body is quite refreshed from ecstasy. At the cellular level there is a vibration and a cleansing and a healing. You do not have to push ecstasy aside. It will pass when it passes.

The ecstasy you have experienced is beautiful, and yes, it passes and reveals that which is even deeper. If there is any idea that any state, even ecstasy, is the limit, then that state is the problem.

Also, you do not have to push pain aside. It will pass when it passes. Then pain and ecstasy are not seen as different.

Pain itself can be very cleansing. It may also feel like the body cannot contain pain, and yet every cell can be cleansed by relaxation into pain.

• • •

I've had several glimpses, and in those experiences, there is a state of total relaxation. It is almost biological for me, like a lightening bolt and a connection to everything. But as soon as there was an awareness of a "me," I was my old self again, and the experience left.

As soon as there was the thought, "*I experienced this,*" or, "*Now I have got some thing,*" the state of relaxation left. This is the clue that some *thing* is being defined as *I*. The moment that the *I* thought arises, there is some tension. There is an image or sensation, some limitation or definition of "me." If there is identification with definition, there is something to defend. There is something that has been lost that must be regained. Then, as you say, you as the "old you" is back. This is always the result of following the *I* thought outwards toward definition. In this case, the definition is *I* who am connected to everything, then, *I* who have lost that connection.

If the *I* thought arises and you turn your mind to see *I*, rather than attending to the definitions that follow *I*, you will see it is nonexistent. It is simply a thought arising. The habit of following or rejecting or denying this *I* thought, is once again revealed to just be activity of the mind. Do you follow this?

Yes.

Good. Because I am speaking to that which saw through the *I* thought. That which relaxed attention on the *I* thought and actually saw that the *I* you have defined yourself as, is illusion.

There is no need to mourn the loss of any experience, even the loss of the lightening bolt experience. In mourning that apparent loss, there is clinging to the idea of the experiencer as some real entity separate from consciousness.

If I would ask anything it would be, is there a way to always experience that let-go?

You ask for a way, but every way is some attempt or some strategy to either reject something or cling to something. Simply let go all strategies—all attempts to hold, and all attempts to keep away. However, letting go is not the correct terminology because this too implies an activity. The secret is more subtle even than letting go. The secret is to discover, in fact, *who* is holding on. It is that simple.

I understand that it may not seem simple because we are conditioned and fixated on either pushing aside, ignoring and denying, or chasing, searching, and clinging. You know that none of these really give you what you want. The more you try to reject or deny or ignore some phenomenon, the more it has a hold on you. The more you try to chase or search or cling to some phenomenon, the more it escapes you.

I called it biological because it seemed to just happen to me. I didn't do it.

Calling it biological limits the phenomenon to somehow being initiated biologically. Definitely biological events follow Self-recognition. The lightening bolt, the energy, the sensations follow, but this that I am pointing to is before biology, includes biology, and is after biology.

Permanence is who you are. The relative identification of yourself as a person, and of yourself as something that glimpses truth, and of yourself as something losing the glimpse, all occur within the absolute truth of who you are. For an instant the ocean can recognize itself within the form of a wave.

The ramifications are endless. The manifestations are endless. The byproducts are-endless. But the basic, absolute truth is simple beyond imagination. That is how it is a secret.

• • •

So, no matter what the experience, pleasurable or unpleasurable, allow it to come, allow it to go?

The truth is, even "allow" is too much effort. It comes. It goes. Allowing is closer than resisting, but to *really* allow is to let go of both resisting and allowing.

You are that which sees. See. The experience is deeper, newer, and fresher every moment. The moment you cling to any experience as reality, you are attempting to resist. With the attempt to resist, you experience yourself as back in the cycle of reaching for something you think should be happening or rejecting something you think should not be happening.

There is great beauty and depth of experience in being willing to experience bliss, joy, and happiness. Also, great beauty and depth of experience are available in directly experiencing pain, grief, and despair.

Many people turn from grief and pain, but many also turn from bliss and joy. There is fear of pain and grief, and there is fear of bliss and joy. With any fear, there is the impulse to contract.

Have the willingness to simply be. All experience follows beingness. When this simple fact is recognized, the depth of experience is unimaginable. In the willingness to experience the perfection of pain, and in the willingness to experience the perfection of joy, there is such depth of understanding that finally, you cannot find a boundary between pain and joy. You cannot say *this* is more joyful than *that* because in the willingness to fully experience whatever arises, you find that which is immeasurable.

Sex and the True Meaning of Tantra

Merging is an exquisite experience that reflects truth. Merging is the teaching of true Tantra. Not sexual activity but the recognition of non-separation between yourself and everything. The real meaning of Tantra is the recognition that true *I* is uninterrupted, pure, pristine, untouched consciousness and cannot, in truth, be interrupted by any perception, any illusion, or any appearance of other.

The problem with the concept of merging is that it presupposes there was, in reality, some separation to begin with. Merging, as sublime as it is, is already one step into the story of separation.

Sex can be beautiful. Touching can be beautiful. But when fulfillment is associated with some cause and effect concept of sex or touching, suffering is created. Then the physicality of sex is an obscuration to truth.

Deep longing for intimacy must be realized. Don't miss the opportunity to experience this longing directly, with no action taken to satiate it. Then the longing can speak. Love can speak to Itself.

True intimacy is endless. It has nothing to do even with human beings. It is an intimacy with the whole universe. This is the real meaning of Tantra, the true meaning of Tantra. It is an embrace of the universe in all of its horror and all of its beauty—in love with that, embraced by that, intimate with that. This is Self-love.

• • •

I have been confirming my sexuality at a deep level. I am trying to just let it be there and not act it out. You make it sound so easy, but for me it's so intense.

Yes, it can be very intense.

I've been trying to contain it, and there is warfare going on inside me.

The point where it becomes quite easy is when you are actually, directly experiencing it. It is the approach to that direct experience that can seem very difficult because of the deep conditioning to do something with this enormous sexual force.

I have been seeing how much sexual desire is wrapped in my mind, and how much the thoughts whip it up.

Yes, fantasy. Some people, after realizing how much the mind is entangled in sex, are no longer interested in sex because they are no longer interested in feeding the mind. This is not true for everyone, but for some people it is.

Right! I've found that here in satsang, I can watch sexual thoughts come, and I can just dissolve them into that spaciousness. I can laugh at them and say, "No, I won't go for that."

I read somewhere that one of the qualities Papaji liked about you was your chasteness. For me, this is a first glimpse of what chasteness might be.

Chasteness is a state of mind. It means to be open and unsoiled. It is not that sexuality is necessarily unchaste. Although some sexuality is very soiled, dirty, and distorted, sexuality can also be pure and pristine.

I want to correct one thing you said about dissolving sexual thoughts. You said that you can dissolve them into spaciousness. But you don't need to dissolve them. If sexual thoughts are not fed, they dissolve effortlessly.

Obviously, an enormous mind-play revolves around the sexual dance. Sex is where most people experience some bliss, some release, some silence, some peace. In linking up bliss and silence and peace with the sexual act, there is recurring generation of struggle, tension, acquisition, and loss. Many people will say that sex is as good as it gets, and they are quite willing to perpetuate the sensual chase.

In the moment of sexual release, there is an explosion the body cannot contain. There is the revelation of nobody, nothing, a vast peace. This is the end of the searching and the tension. The truth of what always *is*, is revealed. The problem arises when sexual intimacy is named as the source of this revelation. Sexual intimacy is not necessary to discover the deepest intimacy, to discover peace with no cause.

If you are actually more interested in pristine, pure, immaculate peace than in what has been imagined will give you that peace, then as sexuality arises and dissolves, it points you towards that peace.

Sexual repression is another example of distortion in the hope of liberation. If repression worked, the group in India called the Nagas, who cut off their genitals so they would not have to experience the sexual force, would all be enlightened, but they aren't. They are eunuchs.

I am not recommending repression. However, in our Western culture in particular, we have worshipped sexual power. We have worshipped it, followed it, fed it, bowed to it, and ultimately been enslaved to this sexual tyrant. If you follow sexuality with thought and energy and devotion, you are following a limited god. When limited gods are worshipped, the devotees suffer.

The peace that is revealed in the moment after orgasm—where there is no you, no other, just vast limitless space—is *already* the truth of who you are. It is always and already present. You can immediately surrender to that vastness with no need of the sexual dance. Then you will not assume that somebody or some act is needed for fulfillment or bliss. All that is needed is to recognize who you already are. Experience that directly, and sexuality takes its rightful place as follower, not as leader.

See through the sexual game, and you will recognize the source that sexual energy arises from and dissolves into. Then sexuality is in its rightful place. Then it is possible to be pure, to be chaste. Then it is possible for sex not to cause suffering.

Peace is not about acquiring other sexual experiences or other sexual partners. Peace is about realizing that you are already at peace. You are already fulfilled if you will but recognize the truth. Whether or not you ever have sex again, discover the truth of your nature and you are fulfilled.

People get very afraid of the thought of never having sex again. Liberating this thought cuts the bondage of the belief that without sex your life would be dead or meaningless. If you are bound to sex for your meaning, your life *is* meaningless. Discover true meaning in that which has no need of anything for its meaning, that which has no need of form, no need of name, no need of unformed, no need of unnamed.

The revelation of not needing anything is the truth of your being. You have the potential to discover that, to realize that yourself. Not just hearing it said, but to directly discover it yourself. Then the tendencies of repressing or indulging no longer have the power to cause re-identification with suffering. They are only powerful prior to direct experience.

Repression is not freedom, but neither is what gets called expression. What gets called expression is usually some kind of childish acting out as a means to acquire pleasure. The treasure is revealed in neither repressing nor acting out. In non-action, there is no work for the mind. In either repressing or acting out, there are the thoughts, *I am doing this. I am getting this. I am keeping this. I am avoiding this. I am ignoring this.* With no mental movement toward or against, there is no work for the *I* thought.

Give the mind no work, and see what remains. See for yourself. Investigate. Experiment. What have you got to lose? You can always go back to worshipping the god of sex. Our culture certainly supports it. Turn on the television, open a magazine, walk down the street, look at men's, women's, and even children's fashions, and you see that sex is worshipped. You can always re-stimulate the sexual chakra if that is where your interest is. Just as an experiment, why not see what is deeper than that. See what has always been chaste, has always been pure, what cannot be defiled.

• • •

I spend a lot of my energy in the area of lust and the pre-occupation with lust. Also, I am a gay man and I have a lot of trouble with my sexuality and feeling good about myself.

Don't even identify yourself as a man, much less a gay man. When a man recognizes he is not a man, this recognition is liberation.

In identification as a male body with particular hormones coursing through it, and with the onslaught of our cultural conditioning and stimulation, the usual course of action is to either hate or to be devoted to that identification.

This holds true for any gender or any form of sexuality. Identification is the distraction. Come back to the beginning, before you were told and before you believed, *I am a man.* When you roll back all your thought processes to before you even identified yourself as a person, what distraction do you find there?

There is no distraction.

Yes! And this is present every moment. Everything that follows is what you have been told, or what you believed, or what you read, or what your ancestors were told. It gets factored into the DNA, and identification becomes the preprogrammed, usual course of action.

You are pure, undifferentiated consciousness. All name and form and sub-name and sub-form are secondary and ultimately irrelevant to that pure consciousness. If you identify with the secondary and irrelevant, there must be some suffering because it is false identification. When you identify with the source of everything, there is no distraction with the false. The source is present every moment because it is unborn and therefore not subject to death.

Source has been named Eternity or God or Truth. Whatever name your culture has tried to put on it, Truth is untouched by any name. It is before name. You are That which is before name. Recognize yourself as who you are, and see that no seductive identification can give you that. Self-recognition of source is joy beyond belief. This recognition makes pleasure, sexual or otherwise, pale. There is nothing wrong with pleasure, but it simply does not touch the joy of realization of the source.

Now, with your attention on the fullness of *before distraction*, see if anything is lacking here, if anything is needed.

Nothing is needed.

Now you have stopped the momentum of all past desires. It is the sweetest irony. When you are willing to die to all distractions of desire, fulfillment is revealed.

Continue to discover what is before the first identification.

• • •

I have been accused by some of sinning for my sexual actions. What is sin? Does it exist?

Sin means mistake, dire mistake. The original sin is the mistake that you are separate from God. In the play of the mind, there is horrible sinning. There is perpetuation of harm and suffering. All sins come from the original sin. In following the perception of separation as reality, fear and then grasping—greed and lust—arise. When these are thwarted, hatred and rage arise. Sex often plays a major role in this familiar tragedy.

My sin was fornication.

If it causes suffering, then it is a sin, it is a mistake.

Sometimes people take freedom to mean license for the physical body. While there is the experience of relative freedom for the body in terms of physical circumstance, there is no possibility of absolute freedom for the physical body. Stop searching for everlasting freedom with the body. The physical body is imprisoned by the forces of nature. There is no way out. The emotional body is imprisoned in feelings of "me, me, me." The mental body is imprisoned in thoughts of "why, why, why." True freedom is not about freedom of body, mind, or emotion. It is about recognizing what is beyond and untouched by body, mind, and emotion.

If you are no longer identified with the body needing its freedoms, or the emotions needing their freedoms, or the mind needing its freedoms, then you realize absolute, everlasting freedom.

• • •

Recently, I have been trying to find all the places where I get pulled away from what I really want.

I have a woman's body, and she wants sex, she wants love, she wants chocolate or whatever distraction. In this, there has been an immediate recognition of how all things just come and go, all kinds of sensual pleasures, and there is a turning back in and asking, "What do I really want?" I want to feel bliss, love, joy, and a remembering that this is already here. It's really beautiful because then there are still all the joys of sensual life but without the disappointment of being pulled away.

I would make one caution. When you say, "the joys of sensual life," you designate sensual pleasure as the cause for joy. Causeless joy is within you, whether there is sensual stimulation or not. As long as there is any misunderstanding that joy is outside you in some object, then there is identification with body and sensuality and the outward activity of the mind. When there is recognition that joy is within, untouched by anything, then there is the recognition that true joy has no need of sensual pleasure, and the mind ceases its outward activity.

All objects begin and end, and in that, there is usually some disappointment because they can't be maintained.

The disappointment arises when they are given the title, "That's Where My Joy Is," because this is a lie.

When I follow peace and bliss and feel calm within, suddenly a vibration starts in my whole being, and it is as if I'm walking around in an orgasmic experience that doesn't end.

You have recognized that what you want is here already. You have recognized the futility in these habits of reaching for *It* out there in some object or some different activity. This recognition is maturity.

In certain lifetimes sensual passions are very strong. Genetically, culturally, there may be very strong identification with passions. It is wonderful in a lifetime when this strength is turned back to that which is the true passion. Then there can be an ever-deepening realization of truth.

In the recognition of true passion, sexual neurosis is then obliterated by sacred gratitude.

• • •

I'm finding that sex just doesn't do it anymore. It doesn't take me to that peaceful place where I'm feeling satisfied and happy. In fact, nothing's doing it anymore.

Excellent. Now you don't even have hope.

Sleep also doesn't do it anymore.

As you say, nothing does it.

Isn't there something that does it? I would pay any price for this.

Will you really pay any price? Because this is what it finally gets to. What price is willing to be paid?

Are you willing to give up your search for it?

My search has led me this far.

Sex led you so far. Sleep led you so far. Whatever else you had thought "did it" for you led you so far.

So where do I go from here?

What if you stop? What if you don't reach for another experience? What if you are actually still? Not still so that you will get something—stillness to get something is not stillness. Really stop. Give up hope.

I am not asking that you pick up hopelessness in place of hope. Hopelessness is just the other side of hope. Give it all up. Are you willing to pay that price? I know your stories of what has brought you here so far, but now you are here, and here is too subtle for any vehicle that brought you here. You cannot drive any vehicle into here, however well it has served you. It is too gross.

You must be willing to pay everything. Give up your defeats. Give up your victories. Give up your worthlessness. Give up your arrogance. Give up your non-importance. Give up your importance. Give up what you know, and give up what you don't know. This is the price required.

How?

By not picking any of it up, and if you pick any up, drop it immediately. By recognizing that what you are giving up is only the poison of false identification.

That brings up a lot of fear inside me.

Now that the protective barrier has been crushed, fear is revealed.

Where is the fear? Where do you perceive it?

Right now, physically, I perceive it here in my gut.

From the core of the fear in your gut, see the reality of this fear. Not honoring where you imagine it to be, not honoring its boundary, not honoring its story—give up that honoring. Go into the core of this and see what it really is.

What do you find?

The fear of letting go of everything that I am.

Now you are honoring some story about this fear. Drop that. You have given that up, remember? Don't take it back. Speak from the core of fear itself. Not some story about fear, not an evaluation of fear, not a definition of fear. Drop deeper than your commentary about fear. This commentary pays obeisance to fear as a god. It keeps fear imagined to be real, keeps fear experienced as reality.

In other words, don't intellectualize it so much?

That's right. Do not intellectualize it at all. In this moment, at least, simply relax. Then you have the capacity to experience this that you have defined, this that you have analyzed, and this that you have been haunted by. I am asking you for one second to stop all mental activity, to be absolutely still. In that stillness, you are at the core of what was previously defined as fear. Since you perceive it somewhere in your belly, put your consciousness into the center of that, into the core of that.

I feel more fear, then the fear starts to go away.

Yes. Then feel even more fear. There must be a willingness to feel what has never been felt. I am not talking about the willingness to dramatize what has never been felt, or intellectualize what has never been felt, but to directly experience what has never been felt, to be willing to experience that more and more.

If I relax and feel what I'm feeling, it's not so bad.

Not so bad is a good beginning. Now relax more. Relax completely. Let go of everything. You need do nothing. Discover what is already here, what has always been here in the heart of the fear.

I feel at peace.

Yes. There is peace. You cannot *do* peace. Nothing can do that for you. It just *is*.

• • •

I am observing that so much of the sexual energy is in the mind. Once one relaxes into being, sex does not seem so important. I find this worrying, and maybe this worrying is just a fear of leaving the past behind.

You fear leaving the sexually identified past behind. Our whole society says that if you leave sex behind, you are gone, you are nothing. When you realize you are already nothing, sex does not seem so important!

If one acts from a place of no-mind, does sex also happen, or is sex always dropped before enlightenment?

Sexual desires arise. Sexual desires cease. If sexual desires arise again, sexual desires cease again. What is the big deal? It is really, inherently, not such a big deal. It has been made a big deal by our society and by our fears that if sex goes, it means the end of joy.

It's not a question of dropping sex before enlightenment. That would be similar to the idea of dropping hunger, or some other natural phenomenon before enlightenment. What must be dropped is false identification. Drop your identification as sexual being. Return to original being. Then sex as phenomenon is no problem.

Can one be Zorba the Buddha, living totally in the world, enjoying all the pleasures and delights as an enlightened being, or do you perceive this as an impossibility?

If you model yourself after anybody, there is big trouble. If you emulate a model, you then have an idea or an image of what enlightenment looks like, of what enlightenment acts like.

You can model the freedom and the surrender of both Zorba and Buddha, and you can then see how that manifests in this phenomenon you have named yourself. But if you look at the Buddha and think that enlightenment must mean no sex, or if you look at Zorba and think that freedom must mean a certain amount of sex, then you are missing the mark. It is these models that cause the comparisons and feed further mind activity.

What if you do not look anywhere, for any model, and simply be as you are?

Beingness is primary. Sex is secondary. Recognize yourself as this that is primary, and let secondary be secondary. If you are not focused on sex as "should be" or "shouldn't be," you will see whether sex is appropriate, or if it is ever appropriate again. Then, it is simply clear.

• • •

It was a real shock when I once heard you say, "Imagine never having sex again." I could imagine dying in this instant rather than never having sex again.

Then for you, this is dying. Do you see?

If you imagine that your sex is more important than your very life, then you are bound by sexual fixation. I am suggesting that you imagine the opposite polarity. Imagine your worst fear. If imagining that you will never have sex again is worse than death for you, then you have inadvertently stumbled onto the key for your freedom. Now, I suggest that you imagine that you will never again participate in the sexual act. Imagine yourself paralyzed, castrated. Imagine performing the sexual act to be impossible for you.

Imagine that you can never again do what you want to do. See how you have identified your body, your experience as an incarnated being, to be the source of fulfillment. In identifying the body to be the source of fulfillment, when you witness aging or hormonal change or whatever debilitating shifts of the body, there is great suffering.

Imagine and experience death—sexual death, physical death, emotional death, and mental death. Imagine your worst fear. Let it come so that you can meet it, so that you can finally realize you are truly and completely fulfilled by the very nature of beingness. You are fulfillment itself. Consciously recognize yourself as this fulfillment.

With realization, for some people, there is no more sexual desire. For some people, there is sexual desire that arises but no desire to act on it ever again. For some people, sexual desire arises, and there is acting on it.

You cannot formulate the face of an enlightened being. There is no face. It is in the formulation of enlightenment, or of fulfillment, or even of satisfaction that worrying and suffering arise.

See if there is some knot of identification with fulfillment from the pleasure of sex. True fulfillment is more profound than pleasure.

Please don't misunderstand me. I am not against sex. I am just simply not *for* it.

At a time in my life, I too worshipped sex. I understand this phenomenon of our sub-culture, this off-shoot of the Sixties and Seventies and the reaction to our parents' generation's repression of sex and denial of sexual joy.

I too pursued sex. I experienced great, deep pleasure, ecstasy and merging, and I identified myself as the seeker of that. But through that identification, I also began to recognize, *Wait a minute. However many times I experience merging, however many times I play the whole sexual dance, there is something missing here in my search for truth and fulfillment.*

In the same way, I searched for myself in being identified as a mother. I searched for myself in being identified as a healer. Each time I had to see that there was something missing. Yes, there were great pleasures in all of those, certainly there was a sense of satisfaction, but there was still yearning that I couldn't quite satisfy through any activity I knew.

That is when I said, "I want to be free. Whatever it takes, I will give. I want to be free. Give up my job? . . . Okay, job gone. Give up my identification as healer? . . . Healer gone. Give up my identification as mother? . . . Gone. Give up my identification as sexual being? . . . Gone. Give up my identification as this body? . . . Gone."

What is revealed is what cannot be given up—the absolute truth of who you are. The truth that has been here all along, through the experience of being a baby, through the experience of being a teenager, through the experience of being an adult, through the experience of sexual being, parent, teacher, healer, even person at all. By giving up all identification *whatsoever*, true fulfillment, waiting for discovery all along, is realized. A satisfaction beyond sexual satisfaction, as joyous as that may be, beyond parenthood, as joyous as that may be, beyond witnessing someone feeling better, as joyous as that may be—the satisfaction of needing nothing, fulfillment in itself, overflowing.

Parents and Children

Obviously, children need directing. They need some conditioning. But when you point to that which is untouched by conditioning, then certain skills, like how to use a fork, how to look both ways to cross a street, how to be in a public place, how to be a doctor, a lawyer, a parent, a teacher, are all recognized as secondary to who one is in the depth of Being. This pointing is what a true parent gives to children.

• • •

The one excuse I've believed to be between myself and freedom is my child. It feels like I can't be free and be responsible at the same time.

Yes, this is the great fear. Isn't this a joke? We have looked at freedom as being freedom of the body, and we imagine freedom of the body as the following of the desires of the body. And yet, we know that following personal desires is very often narcissistic indulgence. As you know, bondage to personal desires causes enormous suffering.

What is inherently free is who you are. Who you are does not *become* free. It *is* free. In recognizing this, there is naturally the ability to respond. Before that, responsibility is a concept of duty or of something to be shouldered. It may be tempered with love and care, but it is also something to be borne. Therefore, your child becomes an objectification, a separation between you and that which you really are. This is a deadly joke. You are this very child! Recognize this and you are not searching around for personal freedom. Then nothing can be an intrusion.

Your child crying or exhibiting infantile behavior may not be pleasant. I am not advising you to foolishly smile and say, "How precious." But you can recognize that behavior has nothing to do with the inherent freedom of that child. In your clear recognition, you can much easier be a responsible parent. Right action is not usually preconceived action. It is fresh and clear. It is stabilized in the confidence of knowing the difference between learning (a child must be taught!) and being that which is shining, unlearned, inherently in every child—good or bad. Your child will be very happy to receive this transmission.

The duty of the parent is to first transmit Truth, and then to transmit skills of survival, legacy of civilization, and the accumulated lore of a particular culture. Then the child's body will not be experienced as a burden to you or to themselves. Nothing will have to be forced to prove, "I am."

Conditioning can be very useful, but if the conditioning teaches that one is the conditioned, it is a gross mistake, and it results in unnecessary suffering.

Recognize freedom in mother and child, father and child, friend and friend, lover and lover, husband and wife, student and teacher. All these relationships of one Self are to be recognized as refractions of truth. Then let there be useful discipline and teaching and conditioning.

The childish idea of freedom as an expectation of every desire being met comes from the mentality of a two year old. This is not freedom; it is suffering. It is imagining that fulfilling your personal desires will give you freedom. Spiritual maturity is seeing the result of the trap of expecting objects of desire ever to provide what is *truly* wanted.

• • •

Can I ask you something about mothering?

You and your child will teach each other about mothering and childing. In the most unexpected, spontaneous, and mysterious way there is a direct line of communication. Whether it involves vaccinations or school crossings or the transmission of love and beauty and trust. You have nothing to ask me about that. Ask the inner wisdom that abides in your heart and in the heart of the child. It is the same source. If an external authority is needed, let your heart guide you to it.

When I'm with her, everything that you talk about is just right there. She is everything that you talk about. I guess I just

*hope for her that she doesn't have to pretend that she's not
That.*

Don't burden her with your hopes.

You are saying that when you are with her, it is satsang.
What is the real boundary between you and her?

I know there is no real boundary.

When you recognize it is impossible to not be with her,
truth will be transmitted. She will not grow up taking the
appearance of separation as reality.

Isn't this shred of distrust ridiculous in the face of your
experience of the time with your daughter as satsang? If you
feed distrust, it will lead you into speculations of what might
happen to her or might not happen to her, and then you will
be dismayed to discover that your time with her is strained
and awkward. Don't feed and then transmit distrust.

Parenting is a great role in the mysterious play of one Self.
Let it be that. You cannot control it. Don't confuse yourself
as the role you play. Then you are not burdened by mother-
hood, and she is not burdened as "your" child. Play the role
fully and completely *as a role*. Trust your Self.

• • •

*I have a four-year-old son, and I feel he looks to me for
boundaries and for understanding who he is. This is kind of
hard because I don't want to mess him up the way that I've
been messed up.*

Maybe you are not messed up.

Maybe not, but I feel like I am.

Yes, I understand you feel like that, but that is probably because your mother felt that she wasn't going to mess you up the way her mother messed her up. Then "messed up" is the message that gets transmitted.

Then could you give me some advice?

Yes. Relax. As you naturally teach your child what is appropriate behavior and inappropriate behavior, don't add onto the teaching that he is the behavior, that he is "bad" or he is "good." Then perhaps this child will pick up the truth that behavior is simply behavior, and certain behavior is appropriate in certain situations, but he is consciousness Itself.

Before he has any possibility of picking that up from you, you have to realize it yourself. Begin by stopping the story, "I've been messed up."

• • •

You've said how important it is to accept a child for who they are, in the same way that we ourselves want to be accepted for who we are. I've been wondering these last few days about my children coming into adolescence. There is tremendous anger and a pushing of boundaries. They are doing normal teenager stuff, but I don't want to see them do something that might cause serious trouble. It brings up all kinds of questions in me about how to accept them and yet also be a responsible parent.

Responsibility is not found in a formula. It is free and comes from the willingness and the courage to respond appropriately. The appropriate response is unknown beforehand. It cannot be rehearsed.

Most people are still stuck in an adolescent frame of mind. You must discover if there is some of your own unresolved adolescent experience manifesting by wanting it your way. Adolescence is like a larger version of the two year old, only now it is about more power, perhaps a driver's license, and dangerous toys. It is further complicated by the torrent of hormones with their emotional and physiological imperatives.

I don't want to make light of this. The truth is many adolescents do get killed or kill themselves. It is a turbulent time. It is obviously one of the big shifts in life.

Adolescents push parents, and in that push, whatever is unresolved can be seen. If you are willing to actually experience the fear and terror and anger that may be evoked in this relationship, if you are willing to experience these emotions without indulging them and without blaming your children or letting them walk all over you; then there arises an appropriate natural response. It may not always look appropriate, since *natural* often does not conform to *normal*.

True responsibility is intuitive wisdom.

Will that letting go process aid in the child moving through difficult times more rapidly?

Some things cannot be known. You cannot know what it is a child has to resolve in this life. You can only be there as the truest kind of support. True support does not rule with an unloving, iron hand. It doesn't ignore the child. It doesn't say, "Oh honey, sure, whatever you want." It is true to the moment, ruthlessly true.

It is also important to be willing to make a mistake, and to be willing to see when a mistake has been made so that it can be corrected. If there is no willingness to make a mistake, there is no possibility of spontaneity and appropriate action.

But I find that when I'm on my own path, away from my child, I'm able to feel peaceful.

Your child is on your path! Doesn't he show up on your own path?

But it brings up anger and fear and despair.

Yes, of course it does. What can be harder than being a parent or a child? Those are the two most demanding roles to play because they do evoke anger, fear, and despair.

When you are willing to stop practicing your own neurosis, you stop the transmission of neurosis. It is finished, and the finishing is retroactive. It permeates throughout every cell of your ancestry in both directions. Even your child's potential unborn child is affected by your awakening. The acceptance, the willingness to see everyone as they truly are, spreads like a wildfire. It is the truth, and it penetrates through all the disguises and lies. All anyone wants is to be truly seen as they are. That is all your child wants, and that is all you want.

Seeing doesn't mean you have to like his terms. True seeing is to still see him through all the difficulties. When you are seen, then you can see, and seeing gives birth to true responsibility. Not from some textbook, not even from what worked the last time, but freely responding. Isn't this what you want in your life? Don't you want people to respond to you freely, and don't you want to respond to people and events freely?

Yes . . . yes, it is what I want for myself and for him.

You cannot wait for anybody else to see you. First be still, and then see, "I Am, and in That, I am complete." Then you are able to see everyone clearly.

Of course, if you are concerned that your child have a good position in the world, or that he lead a safe, predictable life, that everyone accepts him, then you are simply supporting him as a robot.

I just don't want him to kill himself.

Yes, certainly, but the hard truth is he may kill himself. Before he kills himself, if he does, you can be with him fully, completely, so that his life will not have been a waste. If he lives to be a hundred and five and he has not experienced being seen, and therefore is unable to see, his life will have been a waste.

His life is not separate from your life. He is not an interruption of your life. Parenting is a catalyst that breaks up any crystallized ideas of complacency or comfort or knowing what things will look like. The parent/child drama is a beautiful plan, divinely ordained. It is not meant to be comfortable all the time, even though, of course, many times it is deeply joyous. If played fully and truthfully, it is humbling and heart opening.

• • •

I'm about to become a grandmother again and my son is suffering a lot. He wasn't nursed and so he has a lot of problems.

Don't believe this story about why he suffers. There are plenty of babies who *were* nursed and are still miserable. I hear from many who weren't nursed, yet still they received what they needed most from their mothers. Often what is given with the mother's milk is not nourishing anyway. True nourishment comes from the open heart, not the milk. Most mothers are children, still looking for true nourishment when they have their own children.

Let your story about why he is suffering be finished. It is the past. The sooner you can drop it, the sooner the possibility that he can drop it.

I had a story about my daughter that I used to firmly believe. I had been neurotic and afraid, and I hadn't known how to be with my daughter. Her behavior reflected that, and we had a difficult time for some time. I finally recognized that the entanglement going on with this person I called my daughter was wrapped in guilt. In coming to face the guilt, by some grace, I was able to let the whole story go.

In the joy of release, I took my daughter out for dinner and I said, "I want to ask your forgiveness for all the stupidity that I perpetuated as a mother. I simply want to ask your forgiveness."

She looked at me strangely and said, "You have asked me that about a hundred times. It's over! I forgave you a long time ago."

It was true, yet I hadn't been able to see the forgiveness. I was too caught in my own story of guilt, and I hadn't been able to see her openness. In my story, she was an extension of my guilt, some proof of my failing. The moment that story was cut, I could see her. I could see this being for who she is and not just as some projection of mine. Not as "my" daughter, not as "my" object, but as who she is. Then we could be together.

Guilt is a saboteur, and there is a time to say no. I don't mean to cover the guilt. There may be apologies that have to be made, but let guilt be finished. When the guilt is finished you can directly experience the pain that is under the guilt—the suffering, the loneliness, the fear, and the sadness. In being willing to experience emotions under the guilt, you are willing to get to the basis of the relationship.

I don't know what your relationship is with your son, but you can refuse the relationship with guilt. Guilt is a nasty and abusive relationship. It is a denial of the love that is there and has always been there.

Maybe you don't even like your son. This sometimes happens. But the love that is present is always present because it is really Self-love. The moment you objectify Self as "my" son, the truth is overlooked. Then you begin to believe your object should look a certain way, or act a certain way, or react in a certain way. If the object does not look or act a certain way, you may try to force it. If it won't be forced, you probably will blame yourself or your child. All of this unnecessary suffering is overlooking the truth at the basis of the relationship. Love is the basis, and true love is free. True love is free of objectification.

• • •

When you mention guilt, I feel like it is what keeps me in relationship with both my children and my parents. It must take courage to let it go.

Do you have this kind of courage, even if it means losing the relationship? When it is a distorted relationship, keeping the relationship doesn't necessarily serve truth. You actually serve your children more by severing a distorted tie. Then there is the possibility of coming together Being to Being, not victim and victimizer. This means being willing to lose everything.

Freedom means being willing to lose everything—suffering, judgments, ideas, concepts, expectations, images, experiences, and identification. Guilt cannot exist without all of those components.

Not to accept it?

Do not accept guilt.

It's not the way you can face other emotions?

Guilt is not an emotion.

It covers up all these other feelings?

That's right. Guilt overlays emotions with images and stories and violence—either internal violence or external violence.

Put an end to the violence. You cannot meet any emotion in violence, and guilt is violence. You can only meet in openness.

Guilt is perpetuated, self-inflicted violence. In openness there is no guilt. Peace is in the openness.

Are you saying guilt is a justification for continued violence?

Yes. I am saying to stop this horrible game of torture. Guilt is a learned torture. It is the same with doubt. Guilt and doubt are not pure emotions. They are both deflectors used to keep what is feared from being experienced.

• • •

I would like to share the experience I've had with my mother because it is so beautiful to find that she is not only my mother, but she is much more than my mother. She knows the truth as much as anybody else, and she's so simple.

And who would have expected it there!

Yes! We were both so surprised about that freedom.

What good fortune that this discovery happens while she is still alive. Mother discovers it in child. Child discovers it in parent. Then it is seen everywhere.

Maybe it is obvious that truth is in the ocean. Maybe not so obvious in the little spider scurrying up the wall. Once you clearly see, however, you see truth everywhere. In the tiniest little ant, there you are. It is not by some mistake that this spider appeared in your path. It is not by some mistake that you find yourself in the middle of the ocean. Make good use of all meeting.

Thank you!

Allowing yourself to be seen is the thanks. You are seen, and then you see. Let yourself be seen, and let yourself see. Then you will see through apparent differences. Mother, daughter, father, son, cousin, uncle, spider and ocean— through the differences to what is eternally the same. Then response is natural. It doesn't need to be rehearsed.

• • •

My nine-year-old son has no interest in the academics that he's being pushed into, and yet, there is this culture he has to be in.

I know there is no real rule book for parenting, but I would love to hear you speak about that.

What do you mean, "He has to be in?"

Do you know how upset Ramana's mother was when he ran away from home?

Ah! Yes. Very true!

She came and pleaded with him and begged him to come back home, and he wouldn't even speak to her.

His brother also came and said, "You aren't being responsible. You have a family. You have a culture. Our father's dead, and you are responsible for your part in the family. What are you doing sitting here like this, like a beggar?"

Isn't there a way to do both?

Maybe, but it's not for you to say.

See what it is you finally want for him, what it is you want for him above everything, so that when you are long gone, he will have that.

I want to play the role of parent in a way that supports his development.

In the final say, the best that you can give him is the encouragement to be true to the depth of his being, and the sooner, the better.

The reason people flock to gurus is because they did not have spiritual parenting. I call Papaji, "Papaji," because he refuses to let me be untrue to truth.

Of course, there are differences in styles, personality, propensities, and destiny, but of primary and universal importance is to be true to the truth of who one is.

Ramana wasn't an outstanding student. He liked sports more than anything else. He was versed in religion, but he wasn't a religious pundit, and this is all to our benefit. Because had he been immersed in religion, maybe he would have thought that religious education led to his awakening.

Instead, out of the blue, by some mysterious, causeless intervention, as a sixteen-year-old boy, Ramana was able to directly experience his fear of death, with no one apparently guiding him. It is that innocent awakening that is the promise to all of us here, and all of those who are touched by all of us. Innocent, immediate, causeless awakening. This awakening spreads infinitely.

The challenge is to be true. Being true to the truth of your being is the transmission of truth to your children and everyone else you meet.

We have the example of great gurus, great artists, and great scientists, but the world as a whole, the "normal" world, does not support being true to awakening.

This is the challenge. It is the challenge of a lifetime.

Give your life to that. Give your role of "Mother" to that. Give your son's life to that, your husband's life to that, and then see.

Yes, it is a radical surrender, and it does not exclude conditioning and training, but conditioning and training are secondary to the primary, essential transmission.

I understand. I get it that it's living the truth.

Yes, living the truth!

• • •

One of the questions I still have is how much to talk about the truth with my nine-year-old child?

Don't restrain yourself. As it comes up, be willing to speak the truth. If you fall prey to the temptation to preach, immediately be still. Let truth speak through you rather than you speaking through truth. Speaking is more than sounds made through vocal chords. Speaking is the emanation of your life. Speak silently, and you will speak truly. Live truly, and you respond fully.

If you live satsang, whatever language is spoken is the language of the heart; it is the language of truth. It speaks to and from a nine year old as easily as any other age, because it is alive in any age.

Being in the World

Someone once asked, "What is the difference between surrender to the uncontrollable, unspeakable, unnamable Thatness and being crazy?"

The primary difference is in the words "me" and "my." Even when you speak about "your" realization, the fall into at least mild delusion and craziness has already begun. There is a tinge of craziness in claiming anything as "mine."

When you recognize there is no "me," there is only That recognizing Itself through perception of form, this is real sanity. Not what passes for sanity in the world, but true sanity, bliss of being.

Yes, there can be a fear of being crazy with happiness. Dare to be that happy. Then you will see you are happy because you are nothing! You are no thing at all. You will laugh and laugh. When you laugh, the mind is stopped. In the instant of laughing, there is no thought. In any instant of no thought, your true face is revealed. Live in the world of false faces knowing your true face.

• • •

In that moment of both emptiness and fullness, there is the feeling that nothing matters. If you are in that space, how can you get anything done in the world? Why would you want to work then?

The *idea* that nothing matters is very different from the *experience* that nothing matters. The experience that nothing matters is one of expansion. It is not a nihilistic dismissal of responsibility. If you relegate the experience to the idea of nothing mattering, you miss the mark. In no thought, the concepts *everything matters* and *nothing matters* both collapse.

There is no formula for the manifestation of realization. Ramana stayed at the foot of the holy mountain Arunachala all of his life. He lived the life of a sadhu in retreat from the world, and yet the whole world has been touched. How was that done? Who can say. Looking for a formula or a particular activity for the enlightened life is the attempt to imitate or model space itself. Living by imitation is living indirectly. You are space. Be as you are, and see. See.

So the radiance comes out of just being anything?

Anything. NO THING.

For seekers in India, the life of a sadhu is considered the correct life. A life of abstinence from the world is considered a holy life. In other cultures, the life of total service is considered the correct life. Some truly holy lives will be celebrated by the world. Some will remain obscure and unknown by the world. A true life, a holy life, is one lived in surrender to truth, however it looks.

Stop the practice of separating yourself from totality, and life is fully, unknowingly, mysteriously revealed. You will be quite surprised. Your life may not change at all, or it may change quite radically.

Satsang is revealed in your life-stream. The ocean of truth is revealed in silence, in speaking, in eating, in walking, in sitting, in action, and in non-action.

There is no particular face to enlightenment, no particular personality to enlightenment, and no particular action to enlightenment. Defining enlightenment is not enlightenment. That is somebody's version of enlightenment, and all versions are limited.

• • •

I have questions about living in the world and money. I don't have anything secured toward my future, and I guess there is some fear about that.

This fear has nothing to do with the future; it only has to do with the past. It has been passed on to you. Release the past from your mind, and you recognize it to be truly finished, completely over. Every time a thought or feeling of need arises, or fear of survival, meet it as it is. As long as you are following fear-generated thought with instructions from the past, it may seem to have a kind of respectability. Respectable fear is called worry. It is some heritage maybe passed on to you from your parents who received it from their parents. It is a worthless gift from your ancestors.

Discard this worthless gift. Meet fear directly, clearly. In this direct meeting, you will discover there is really no fear. In that discovery, clarity naturally reveals itself.

I cannot say whether you will have money next week or next year or ever. I can say that if you are willing to meet this fear, whether you have money or you don't have money, you realize you are free. You are free of the bondage of the past.

If you go back far enough in your ancestry, most likely there was the experience of imminent starvation. This is a huge fear, and it gets passed on generation to generation. But look at you. Look at the affluence of this lifetime. Look at the grace of this birth. If you waste this lifetime carrying around the old baggage from five generations ago, you will miss this exquisite window of opportunity to discover what is at the core of this and every fear.

Right now, you most likely have no real worry about your next meal or about your shelter. Of course, you can fabricate many worries if you want a special meal or a better shelter, but I am speaking of the most elementary concerns. In your life at this very moment, there is no real need to worry.

What a rare lifetime! What a good birth. What a moment! Use this opportunity. Don't throw it away. Meet life fully and completely. Discover who you are, *really* who you are.

All of your circumstances support your awakening now. You find yourself in satsang. You find yourself where truth is being spoken directly to you, as you. What an opportunity. As you say, you recognize there is no real problem, and yet you still have this old fear. Now drop all of your mental baggage about fear, and meet it pure and simple. By baggage I mean any concept concerning past, present, or future.

The fear of survival is a deep, animal fear, but the human animal is a rare incarnation. The human animal actually has the possibility to discover its true identity as Beingness Itself. What a mystery. What a gift. I have heard it said that it is possible in other species. I don't know about that, but I know that it is possible in this species to awaken now.

There may come a time in the future when food and shelter are not so certain. There have definitely been times in the past when there was no food or shelter. At those moments of preoccupation with survival of the organism, the question of who you are is usually overlooked.

Here you are without those concerns. Will you overlook this essential question from habitual concerns of survival, or will you now discover the truth?

● ● ●

All my life I've noticed how I constantly go out and come back, go out and come back. I have those moments of real peace and bliss inside myself, but then I go out again.

Where is out, and where is in?

I'm not sure, but it feels out, and it feels in.

Well, let's find out. Let's be sure where *out* is and where *in* is because they are important concepts. Find the boundary between the experience of being *out* and the experience of being *in*.

I can't put my finger on it. I don't know where it is.

That's a good beginning. When you first started talking you were very certain you go *out*, and then you go *in*. First you discovered peace and centeredness and ease within, and then you discovered the inclination of out-in-out-in. This is very important. You discovered retreat. Then you made a separation between retreat and the rest of the time. This separation is only a mental conclusion based on what you believe exists *in* and what you believe exists *out*. In truth, that which is discovered within is not confined to any location. Boundlessness is not limited by any boundaries! Discover peace within, and then see it everywhere. See that in reality there is no in and out. All is in one's Self.

How, then, do I be in the world?

This is the same as the previous question. Stop making the distinction between "me" and "the world." At a certain stage, the distinction of *out* and *in* is an important distinction to make. Discriminating wisdom makes the distinction between what is permanent and what is impermanent, what is real and what is unreal.

However, from what you were just saying, it appears that discrimination has now become institutionalized in your mind. Now you have religious warfare between the *ins* and the *outs*. This familiar, old game is going on only in the mind. The way to end the game is to expose it. Where *in reality* is the boundary between *out* and *in*? I understand feeling *in* and *out*, and experiencing *in* and *out*, but in reality, can any boundaries be found?

At this moment, it is obvious there is no real boundary.

Good. Now, discover what is the real boundary between this moment and any other moment.

• • •

My mind wants to figure it out.

A powerful intellect is a beautiful power, but realization is beyond the power of the intellect to grasp. Realize what gives the intellect its power, and the intellect is humbled, prostrate, floored at the feet of its source. In that prostration, the intellect serves, flowers, and sparkles.

This is the assignment: Speak what cannot be spoken. Speak what has never been spoken. What good use for the vocal cords, for the intellect, for the life experience. Keep the mind totally at the feet of source, so that it may serve that at a moment's notice, and the mind will be divinely used.

I don't know what to say.

That's a good beginning. You cannot know what to say. That is right. Then your mind is humbled.

Don't know what to say. Stay right there.

I am not asking for you to say something in particular. I want to hear what has never been said. I am not talking about words. I am talking about that which uses words. Let It speak for Itself.

• • •

Conceptually I get it about letting go and just being, and also I know that "trying" to be is not being.

It is not that trying to be is not being, because you are still being whether you are trying to be or not. When you are trying to be, you simply have not realized the peace of being without trying, but you still *are*. You cannot say you are not, can you? Even if you say you are not, you can only say you are not because you are!

But what's missing is the realization, the peace. There is still the mind chatter. This internal conversation that keeps going.

Are you tired of this conversation?

Yes.

If you are tired to the degree where you have lost all faith in this god called the commentator, the evaluator, the tryer, then perhaps you will stop paying allegiance to this god. When you stop habitual payment of allegiance, you will naturally and easily recognize these mind games as tricks of a false god.

• • •

One of my biggest fears about enlightenment is that others in the world will judge me.

They will. It is a given. They do right now anyway. Judging is the nature of mind activity, and you are surrounded by that.

Let yourself feel totally judged insane, deluded, absurd, stupid. Whatever it is you imagine will be so hard to bear, let it come now. You will see it is nothing, just judgment. Then what force can it have? Anyway, if they are judging you, they are thinking of you. When you awaken, if they are thinking of you, even if they are judging you, they will receive the darshan of awakening. Let them judge you. It is their way of loving you. Distorted maybe, but at least their attention is on the announcement of awakening.

Invite the judgment. If you directly experience this judgment, if there is any residue of clinging to some particular entity and its status or position in the herd, it will be revealed. Let it be revealed. As long as there is the fear of judgment, there is a sensed lack of freedom to be who you are.

First receive the judgment that you are goodness, you are purity, you are beauty, you are freedom. Fall into that. Then invite the negative judgment. You are stupidity. You are delusion. You are bondage. Now, what is true? Finally, what is true?

Be finished with the prison of others' opinions. You can never acquire a big enough supply of others' opinions to prove that you are goodness, you are truth, you are beauty, if you have not realized it yourself.

There is a story of a man who attended Ramana Maharshi while he was living on the mountain in a cave. At first there were just the two of them, but eventually other people began to be attracted to Ramana.

After eleven or so years of silence, Ramana started speaking. More and more people began to gather around Ramana, and then his attendant began getting possessive, even ordering Ramana around. Finally, he even told Ramana, "This is my cave; this is my ashram." At that time Ramana left the cave. He went down the mountain to where his mother was buried, and a bigger ashram was born.

Eventually the attendant followed him and took over the management of the new ashram. Because he was possessive and generally obnoxious, he generated a lot of strife. Ramana invited his brother to come in and manage the ashram, and the obnoxious man was ousted.

The man was furious and vengeful. One of the things he did was publish a book about all of Ramana's faults. Ramana asked for the book to be brought to him. In the preface to the book was written, "This book would have been much longer, but I ran out of funds."

Ramana saw this and said, "Oh please, we must raise funds for this man." Then he read more of the book and said, "He doesn't know the half of it! We have to get more money, and then we will put this man out in front of the ashram, and he can give these books away to whoever comes."

This is the way to deal with judgment.

I am afraid that others will judge me if my path changes too radically in their eyes.

To be bound by concerns of what others will think—if you are original, if you are true, if you are intoxicated with God, if you are free, if you look strange to them, if you don't keep within the bounds of what they say you should be doing and thinking—is a sad state of imprisonment.

Everyone can relate to this. It is brainwashing and conditioning, and it obstructs satisfaction. No matter how much approval you receive, there is never enough, because true happiness does not depend on the approval of others.

You may even be hated for awakening to the truth. Certainly, some people will hate you for it. It is a threat to their neat, little lives. When I was first with Papaji, a friend got upset with me. She hated me. I was shocked! How could this be? She was my spiritual friend. I asked Papaji about it and he said, "It is to be expected. It is just to be expected."

You will also be adored and loved. Believing either the hate or the adoration is a trap. Don't take either one personally. If you are adored, it has to do with the adoration that is arising in the heart of the being in front of you. If you are hated, it has to do with the deep threat that is perceived and feared within the mind of the being in front of you. This is none of your business. Be true to who you are, radically true to who you are, blissfully, unknowingly true to who you are, and all is taken care of.

Why not just go to a cave and sit?

The cave is within your heart. Go there and sit. Rest there for one second. You cannot rest if you are immediately thinking, *But if I go there, what might happen with my friends, my job, my work, my life?* These are the thoughts that keep you from what you want most.

• • •

I live in the country, and being in nature day in and day out has become a path of mirroring, a way of experiencing life. When I'm quiet and just sitting, all of a sudden I start opening to the nothingness. That is a very peaceful place, and I just watch without judgment, but as soon as it is time to stand up to do a physical action, it's gone.

What is the problem with that?

I have lost the feeling that—

What hasn't been lost? What is present before the feeling, during the feeling, and after the feeling?

Well, peace is.

Is the peace separate from the activity?

When I totally lose the peace is when a human being walks towards me. All of the habits, conscious and unconscious, come up even though I'm just standing there, because a human being has walked into my field.

Yes, it is so hard for humans to recognize other humans as part of nature. You have identified yourself and others like you as separate from nature, as separate from the totality of being.

Particularly when my mind is going click-click, and contraction is happening. It's like a bomb's gone off.

Yes, it is not so subtle.

And this other person and I haven't even started talking yet.

But you have. You started talking long before any actual physical conversation. This human aspect of nature has triggered all of your old superstitious thinking of what human is, what this human reminds you of, and what this human might be. This internal talk is in relationship to yourself and other as somehow separate from the totality of experience.

Nature is your satguru speaking to you, teaching you, parenting you, and being intimate with you in the most impersonal way. Learn the lessons of nature. When these so-called others like you reappear, you will see only your Self in all your infinite form, just as you see infinite form within nature.

Nature is experienced as completely relational, totally present, but not personal. When a tree relates to you, it relates totally but impersonally. You could drop dead and the tree would not cry. This is the great darshan of nature.

I also lose my peace when I have to meet some time agenda. All of a sudden I think, "Oh my gosh, I have a three o'clock appointment and . . ."

That's right. That is an example of taking it personally. The crux of suffering is taking everything personally. Finally, you have to discover who you are. This *I* who is late for an appointment. Where is this *I*?

• • •

When I am out in nature, I am able to drop the sense of feeling separate and recognize myself in everything and every-thing in me. Then I get around people and I start feeling separate again.

It is a common mistake in identity to see nature as some-thing other than or separate from people.

• • •

How do I live with uncertainty?

Really live! Any certainty is only within the mind. When you live in peace with uncertainty, you are naturally confi-dent. Recognize the unknown as the reality of living, and you won't be distracted by thoughts of grasping and trying to make permanent what is by its own nature impermanent. Every event, every experience, every *thing* is impermanent. This recognition is divine uncertainty. It reveals divine security.

• • •

If I become more of that which I am, can I help to heal the world?

This idea of you becoming more of what you are, or of the world becoming something different, is nonsense. You are what you are. Stop all these ideas and beliefs and thoughts, and discover what you are. This is primary.

Discover who you are. Don't become more of who you are. Becoming more of who you are is imaginary. Discover who you are now, and tell me if you can find any location, any boundary, any limit, or any thing that can "become" that.

You have assumed there is something else needed, but this assumption is based on your past idea of what the world is, who you are, what you are becoming, what healing is, who can heal what, and even what enough is. Who is measuring that, and by whose standards?

There is something vast, unknown, and unseen, where measurements of enough are left behind. Here there is no possibility of measuring and no measurer. There is no world separate from who you are. There is only wholeness itself. Nothing becomes whole. It is recognized to be already whole. Recognize that.

But the world doesn't seem whole.

I understand that the world doesn't seem whole. I am not speaking about seeming. Many things seem one way or the other, and this seeming changes back and forth. Something seems one way one day, and within hours it can seem the other way. A cloud goes in front of the sun, and it seems the sun has disappeared. In the night sky, you see stars. In the day sky, it seems the stars have disappeared. In the desert a great lake may seem to be just over there. Drink from that lake and you discover it is sand. Drinking sand is believing "seems."

Seeming is ultimately unreliable, because it is based on sensory information. Seeming is the interpretation of the world through the senses and the conclusions based on past interpretations. Has it been reliable?

The senses are fickle, having to do with moods, biochemistry, genetics, and environmental events. Sensory information is changeable, and if you rely on what is changeable in searching for wholeness, I am afraid you will be searching endlessly. If you can recognize what is already whole, then you have recognized a very deep secret that is always untouched by changes and seemingness.

Recognize what is permanently whole, what is permanently here, and then your lifetime is no longer spent spinning and searching in seemingness.

You know this from your life experience. One set of beliefs is pushed aside for a new set of beliefs, and now the world is seen through the eyes of the new beliefs. Then that set is pushed aside for another set. You read the paper and the world seems one way. You hear another opinion and it seems another way.

I agree with you. But are you saying that the world is fine the way it is?

I am not saying that the world is fine. I am pointing to what is eternally whole. Before that discovery, any conclusion about either the world's fineness or its rottenness is speculative.

You follow the senses as if they give you real, true, accurate information. Obviously they don't, do they? Isn't it all tempered? You take a walk, you feel good, and everything looks good. You take a walk, you feel bad, and everything looks bad. There is a way to see that sees through what looks good and what looks bad, a way to see wholly. But this discovery must come from direct experience, or it is an imposition. Without direct experience, it is just another belief of the latest dogma.

Don't wait for someone to tell you how the world is or what the world is. Only settle for first-hand discovery. Don't wait for some leader to herd you into a particular direction. Even if you believe it is the best direction, you must not settle for anything less than the direct experience of what exists deeper than the senses, deeper than thoughts, deeper than feelings, deeper than conclusions, deeper than the way you have put it all together. Of this, I cannot speak a word. I have yet to find a word that comes close. I can only point you in that direction.

• • •

In the world of samsara, I feel like I lose sight of the truth because I'm occupied from the minute I wake up to the minute I go to sleep at night.

You cannot lose truth. It is only possible to imagine yourself separate from it. This imagining creates samsara. Truth is always present.

I guess I really know that.

Don't even know it. That is the catch. Truth can be attended to, but not as an *it*, not as an object. Truth cannot be known, and when you stop trying to capture it with the mind, there it is. Even samsara cannot exist without truth.

Truth is everywhere, in everything, and if you are paying attention to that, you see it everywhere, in everything. Truth doesn't live in a place. All places appear in truth. If all places appear in truth, then they are of truth.

When I say *attend* to truth, I am not instructing you to focus your mind on something. To focus is to bring to a point. Total attention is three hundred and sixty degrees.

It seems like there's really nothing to do.

Living truth does not have anything to do with activity or non-activity. There is no thought of making anything happen or of not making anything happen. Those thoughts come from fear. They arise from the fear of emptiness, or the fear of nothing, or the fear of nothing happening.

There may arise the desire for a certain outcome. To live in truth is to surrender this desire and put that surrendered attention on the truth that always is.

Then how do things happen?

Quite naturally, just as they always do. What is removed is the struggle. Your natural state is ease of being.

Some people have an idea that enlightenment is some kind of zombie state. You often see a manifestation of this idea in spiritual groups. A kind of numbing out, modeling nothing happening, pretending as if there is nothing happening. Ease of being cannot be pretended or modeled.

• • •

Could you tell me what you understand prayer to be and how it works? How can I use my focused intention to benefit others in the world and ease their suffering?

You are asking about true prayer, not the usual prayer of acquisition.

I'm talking about when I pray for my brothers and sisters or for the world.

Pray for truth. Pray that truth be known. Pray that all being awaken to its true nature. Then pray to be used by truth fully, completely, without any expectation or need of personal or material gain.

You asked how you could use your intention, but if you imagine that you use truth, then truth is imagined as some object, your object. If you pray to let truth use your body, your mind, your emotions, to let truth actually have your life, to let it direct your life, then all of those previous ideas and agendas drop away. All ideas of what you need to do to be happy are finished.

My intention is that the greatest good is done, but how do I use my intention so that this happens?

What is it you want? What is it you really want?

That we remember who we are.

Your whole prayer is right there. If you really want this, the prayer must be one hundred percent. If you take ten percent off to also want something else, and then another five percent for something else, then you have less than a full prayer.

Yes, make your whole life prayer. The details are not up to you, because who can say how life should look? Visualizing how it should look can only come from some past conclusion based on cultural or political conditioning.

With maturity, this particularizing of wants and desires based on past experience is recognized to be futile. Recognize that you don't know what truth should look like, or how truth should reveal itself. Only know that above everything, you want the truth, as you say, for your brothers and sisters, for your Self.

Let truth write the scenario. Let truth live your life. Truth cannot be visualized, because any visualization is still limiting its manifestation.

Truth is not limited. It is not limited to affluence and comfort. It is not limited to poverty and discomfort. If you are attached to any state or circumstance, you are missing the boundlessness in the fulfillment of truth. If you are fixated on a particular image of what your life should be, or what your brothers' and sisters' lives should be, there is that much energy taken away from the prayer for truth.

Isn't true love about the absence of separation?

It is the absence of the belief in the illusion of separation. It is the recognition of the truth of who you are, regardless of appearance, feeling, circumstance, comfort, or discomfort. If this is your prayer, this is a very serious prayer. This prayer takes enormous resolve. It takes the willingness to surrender your personal suffering. To surrender your personal suffering, you must discover what is the root of personal suffering.

The root of all suffering is the belief and the continual practice of the belief that you are separate from pure, limitless consciousness. That you are a separate entity, and that you are located in a particular body. I am not asking that you substitute another belief such as, "I am God," or, "I am limitless," or, "I am boundless." These too are beliefs. You are bigger than any belief. You are beyond measure.

The strong belief in "me" and "my needs" is the root of all evil. It is a great mistake. It is sin.

Your prayer must begin exactly where you are. You imagine yourself to be a particular body because you sense the body. It feels like you are this body, and it looks like you are this body. I am proclaiming that there is that which is closer than the senses, closer than appearances, closer than feelings. Quite remarkably, That realizes Itself even through this manifestation of appearance of body and separateness.

This is what I mean when I speak of prayer. Realized prayer is not asking for something. In realization, your entire life becomes a prayer of thanksgiving. Satsang is thanksgiving. Give thanks for this moment of revelation. Have your life be a life of thanksgiving which naturally springs from revelation. Then all of life is revealed to be a confirmation of that.

• • •

I want to publish my book. I have desires and hopes of accomplishing something in the world.

When I sit quietly, a lot comes in. I write. I paint. Finally, it's like there has to be an end to quiet. I have to get up and do something with what I am painting and writing.

Who says so?

The part of me that wants to always be on the quest.

If you follow that part, you will always be on the quest. You will always be doing something or imagining you are doing something. You will always stay busy.

This is where I don't get it. There's a missing piece.

The missing piece is the piece that you have yet to surrender.

The truth is, if you stop for one pure instant of Self-recognition, those things may either get done more than you can imagine, or they may not get done. There is no guarantee one way or the other. Your particular life form may be more active than it has ever been, or it may be inactive. What you give up by being absolutely still is the choice of appearing to direct the outcome. A true book comes from absolutely stopping. If a true book is to come through your form, it comes through because it cannot be held back.

It comes through the not-doing?

In music, in art, in literature, in science, and in a full life, there is that which cannot be withheld, cannot be constrained. That which has to be expressed. Your intellect, or your limbs, or your voice, or the techniques you have learned are used by that. Your life is used by that, so give your life totally to that. How it is used cannot be known. Perhaps you will have many books. If they are true books, they will come.

Are you saying that place of sitting, of letting go, of surrendering, is so divine that all these things get done anyway?

That place is already here. It is so divine, it is eternal. It is divine beyond any concept of divine. Surrender all your ideas to that to do as it wishes, as it wills. Truth is far beyond individual will. Individual will is just a spark of that.

You will see your life used, but it may be used by your never moving from your room. Truth is unpredictable and uncontrollable. It is divinely uncontrollable, exquisitely uncontrollable, and undeniably uncontrollable.

We become like a vehicle or a conduit or a vessel?

Recognize your true Self. Stop fighting that you are That. Surrender your intellect to that, and then your intellect is used. I don't know if it will be in books. I don't know if you will ever speak or write again. It is irrelevant. How you will be used is bigger than I can know or you can know. Let the future be as it is: unknowable, blessedly unknowable. Speak and write if the speaking and writing must come, and be silent if no speaking and writing can come.

Ramana sat in one place, and his just sitting continues to shake the whole world. Many people said he shouldn't just sit there, that he should be out in the world doing social action like Ghandi. But something bigger than what either people thought or what he had been taught directed his life. Ramana, in his mastery, only answered them in silence. From the outside, it appeared as though he was doing nothing, that he was inactive. But look, this formal satsang, here, in this time, in this part of the world, is the result of his "inactivity."

If it is the nature of a particular form to be active, let it be active. If it is the nature of a particular form to be inactive, let it be inactive. Compassion is not about the activity or non-activity of the form.

You are That which is the source of both activity and inactivity. In your willingness to be that totally and fully, you cannot help but help. Not by any intention of helping, not by any agenda of helping, but through your true nature as love.

Do you follow this? It is very important. People have such ideas about activity and inactivity. Truth is deeper than any idea. Realize truth. Your hidden question is a question of trust. Trust that silence. Trust that pure love, just for an instant. Then at the very least you stop contributing to suffering.

There is a command that is deeper and closer than can be known, and it is more vast than I am able to speak of. It is exquisite. It is alive, present, spontaneous, and out of your mind's control.

You ask is that all there is to it? There is no end to it. No one has ever reported an end or an all to Self. In the instant of being absolutely still, there is an opening of the mind. There is an opening into eternity.

• • •

I find myself on this roller coaster of emotions, getting very angry, getting very sad. Does that mean that I will never reach the state of the bodhisattva where I can help others in the world?

First of all, the bodhisattva state cannot be reached. It can only be recognized as your preconditioned nature. Sattva is a Sanskrit term meaning tranquil, peaceful. Bodhi means awakened consciousness, awakened heart and mind. This is your original nature. As long as you are identified with the roller coaster of emotions, you are overlooking what is already and always calm and peaceful, what is already awake. You are overlooking the truth of yourself by fixating on your emotions with your thoughts.

The awareness in which the roller coaster is roller coasting is already tranquil and awake, with no rejection of the roller coaster and no clinging to the roller coaster. Recognize this tranquillity, and the roller coaster naturally comes to a halt. There is no juice for it to continue. The passions which were fueling the roller coaster are consumed in the one passion for truth, the passion for freedom, the passion for God.

Without being fed, no *body* can exist—neither the physical body, nor the mental body, nor the emotional body. In Indian society it is customary at a certain age for a seeker to become a sadhu, leading a life of physical renunciation as a way to discover the bliss that is beyond bodily needs.

Here, I am saying to truly *nourish* the emotional body, stop feeding the mental body! Discover the natural harmony of emotions that is beyond mental tyranny. By not feeding thoughts, emotions come to rest in the tranquillity of awareness. When some past pattern of emotionality arises, if thoughts are not fed around it, the pattern can cease.

Papaji was asked to leave Ramana's ashram to go rescue his relatives from Pakistan and then to support them. He said, "No, I don't want to go. That is all a dream. I just want to stay here with you, my Master, at your feet."

Ramana said, "Well, if it is all a dream, then what is the problem?"

So, Papaji was back in the play. Working hard as a mining engineer, he supported a hundred people and held satsangs in the evenings.

What a great gift this teaching is for all of us! There is no necessity to do anything with the body. Truth is much more subtle than that. Let the body be as it is. The body is not the problem. The identification with the body as your Self is the problem. You must discover what is present, clear, pure, and untouched, regardless of emotional state. This is bodhisattva. It is already bodhisattva. If there is an attraction to that, a love of that, a respect of that, then give even more love and respect to that, and see how your body is used.

• • •

Sitting here with you, it is so easy. Outside, it is very often difficult, and there is a lot troubling me.

Where is this *outside*?

Not sitting with you.

Then you must have mistaken me for some phenomenon. Don't limit me to any person. Then you will see the word "outside" makes no sense. The phrase, "not sitting with you," makes no sense. This makes as much sense as saying, "I am not present."

I'm playing my old play.

Stop playing your old play. Part of the old play is following the thought that it is easy sitting here and difficult outside. This very thought gives credibility to the possibility of "outside" and "difficult."

Don't give these thoughts credibility. That is the old play of the past. It may arise out of past momentum, but the moment it arises, don't continue to feed it power. In that moment, let the thought sink back into nothingness. Let it be liberated.

But it seems to be my experience in the world.

Your experience is what the old play is. When this old play arises, don't follow it, and there will be no experience of it. The experience is only perpetuated if you continue to feed it by following these thoughts. In the moment these thoughts arise, or when you discover that you have followed them, let them go. At that moment ask yourself, "Who am I? Who am I, *really?*"

Sometimes I do this, and it is helpful, and sometimes I think there is an effort in it.

When you feel the effort, let go of the effort, and don't ask yourself anything.

Sometimes it just falls down by itself.

In each case the old play is finished. It either falls on its own as you let go of any efforting, or you can direct your mind inward. This old play cannot continue without some effort. Maybe you are quite used to this effort, and familiar effort actually seems easy. Don't believe it. Not believing it is the same as not touching it.

So, it only belongs to the old belief system.

That's right. Past experience belongs to the old belief system. Now you are reclaiming your soul from this past relationship with a tyrant god (the old play) who has been drinking your soul's blood.

That's why I wanted to speak, because I really wish to have this in my daily life.

Yes, truth must be realized to be in your daily life. Don't settle for anything less. In every second that you are willing to inquire, you will discover *I* is always here. *I* is always present. *I* is vast, limitless, pure awareness. You are *I*.

The Fire of Service

The life you are living is giving itself to something. What is your life giving itself to? See what your life serves, and then you have the choice. Do you want to serve suffering, or do you want to serve joy, love, and truth?

What you are serving is where your attention is. Your attention reveals what you are supporting. You are supporting it with your thoughts. You are supporting it with your activities in life. You are supporting it with your hopes. You are supporting it with your frustrations. You are supporting it with a story.

What are you serving? Check and see. Are you serving some idea of who you think you are, or some idea of who you think you were, or some idea of who you think you should be? Are you serving some idea your mother had of you, or your father had of you, or your culture has of you, or your bad experiences, or your good experiences? Or are you serving that which is before all ideas?

Narcissism is the result of serving your ideas and images of yourself. Both positive narcissism and negative narcissism are filled with suffering. Suffering can be disguised as pleasure as well as pain.

You must be familiar with narcissism. It is a hold-over from when you were two or three years old. In each lifetime of being two or three years old, narcissism is reinforced and then nourished throughout a lifetime as an ideal of freedom and power.

The therapeutic community has identified an "inner child." Inherent in the concept of "inner child" is some kind of image. Either an image of woundedness, or an image of power, or an image of freedom, or an image of playfulness. Those are only mental images. If you serve those images, if you bow to those images, whether positive or negative, you must tell the truth about what the results are. Just tell the truth; that is all.

There is an opportunity for your life to be lived beyond "whys" and "shoulds"—beyond subservience to conditioning, and beyond rebellion against conditioning. A life freely lived.

See for yourself. Notice in a day or even in an hour what you are attending. What is it you are supporting? What is it you are feeding? See for yourself.

• • •

My whole life I've had feelings of duty and responsibility and a need to be of service. But there is also a massive fear about whether I'm doing it in the right way, and this in itself has become a block.

Yes, your idea of responsibility is a burden.

True responsibility means the ability to respond. Ability to respond must be free, spontaneous, and intuitive. If it is burdened by the weight of past concepts—what responsibility should look like, what it should feel like, how it should be received—it is not true responsibility. An image or imitation of responsibility is a burden.

True responsibility is joyous. It is the willingness to surrender, to be who you are without any idea of what that is. Yes, some fear may arise in that, but if you meet that fear, you will discover it to be nothing. Serve that fear and once again you are shouldering some idea of duty or responsibility. To be responsible is to be true only to the deepest command of your being.

There is no way of knowing the effect your response will have. Whether you never move off a couch or whether you travel the globe and never stop speaking, whether you are a public figure or a private figure, all are secondary to responding to that deepest command. If you are willing to meet whatever occurs in your responsibility to that command, life is naturally and joyously served. The burden appears when you ignore that command with ideas of what responsibility should look like. Put your burden down. Stop contributing to the burdens of the world. Be true to who you are, and you will quite mysteriously and miraculously be placed exactly where you must be. Then you will know the deep joy of responsibility.

Some people have expressed fear that they won't take care of their children properly if they serve truth. What better gift can you give your children than your awakening? If you are true to truth, the world can receive awakening from you. If you compromise truth, compromise is what your life stands for.

What do you want your life to stand for?

I am not suggesting what the form should be. It honestly doesn't matter. Be a mother, a clerk, or a bum. It doesn't matter. All forms are included in truth. When you are true to truth, truth is transmitted, whatever the form. If your students are to be bums, if your students are to be shoppers in the grocery store, if your students are to be your children, what you will transmit is the truth of your responsibility to the deepest command of your being.

Being true means refusing to cling to any idea of what your life should look like. What freedom! Aren't those ideas burdensome? Perhaps some of them are totally in alignment with truth. You cannot know until you are willing to give up all ideas. Then you will see that what is in alignment has no weight, and what is not in alignment is too heavy to fly with you.

Joyous service is not a burden. If it is a burden, stop. Carrying a burden indicates that responsibility is being dictated by some mental concept. In the joy of true responsibility, service is not for an instant separate from surrender, vigilance, Self-inquiry, and devotion.

• • •

In this play of Leela, when you see yourself in another form, and the form is suffering or confused, what is the best service to the Self?

To be absolutely quiet. Quiet provides the only true help, and from the depths of quietness, either particular action or non-action will naturally arise. No thought is needed for direction. Anything else is involvement in a particular story of suffering. As long as you are involved in the particular story of suffering, you are overlooking what has never suffered. Recognize what is whole and complete, now and eternally. True recognition is the mother of all acts of compassion.

Quiet holds the whole spectrum of behavior. There is a ruthlessness and relentlessness to compassion, as well as a gentleness and lightness. The whole range of experience can serve Self. Be quiet.

• • •

I recognize that what binds me to the world of appearances is a devotion to worrying about the state of the world. A devotion to hating the violence that characterizes much of human interaction. There is a fear that things will get even more crazy if I and many others let go of protecting what we think of as inalienably right.

What you are exposing is really a lack of trust. You fear that if you let go of your thoughts and conclusions, you will be irresponsible, or you will be a vegetable, or you will not fulfill service to human kind, to the planet, to all species.

Your fear is not based on reality. It is based on your devotion to worrying. It is based on devotion to recounting all the times you have trusted your thoughts and emotions and interpretations and have been proven to be mistaken. In that conclusion, you equate thoughts and emotions and interpretations with the truth of who you are.

Thoughts and emotions and interpretations appear in who you are. As long as you identify yourself as any thought, grandiose or lowly, or any emotion, sublime or horrible, or any interpretation, profound or mundane, you overlook that which can be totally, completely, absolutely trusted.

You see suffering. You see how unnecessary most of the suffering is, and you desire to put an end to suffering. This is a beautiful desire. It is a true desire. The mistake comes when you trust your thoughts and emotions and interpretations about how it should be done, what you should do, how much you should do, and what it should look like. These thoughts and emotions and interpretations may arise, yet if you place your trust in the unknowable mystery of perfection, there is a flexibility and openness that is both responsible and creative.

There is no particular formula for how help is given. Look at Ghandi, or Martin Luther King, or Mother Theresa, and you see lives of action, lives of commitment and integrity. Look at the Buddha, or Ramana, or Saint Theresa, and you see lives of contemplation, of inaction. Who is to say one life is right and another life is wrong? As long as you have any idea of what it looks like to serve, you are simply overlooking the opportunity to absolutely trust that the intention to serve reveals the discovery of that which serves. The *how* appears naturally from intention and discovery.

I am familiar with this dilemma. I remember weeping at the impossibility of doing what I saw must be done in the world. I know the worrying. I know the torture and the horror of the way we treat one another. I also know the possibility of surrendering to not knowing, to giving up the idea of how "you" must do it. Let it be done. Let your form somehow be used.

If Mother Theresa thought she should stay in a convent and should live a life of contemplation, what a waste. If St. Theresa thought she should be working with lepers, what a waste.

Give up worrying about what you are doing, and discover who you are. Then see. See if that is not trustworthy. You cannot know by checking your thoughts or your interpretations. You can know by checking That. A life lived from the question, "How can I be used?" not *knowing* how, but continually *discovering* how, is an open life. It is a life that radiates trust in who one is. What a life! A life lived in trust.

Trust is rare, and trust is your opportunity. You are actually in a position to trust. You needn't be concerned every moment with where your next meal is, where your shelter is, or if your family is safe. Not having to be concerned with issues of immediate survival is a great privilege, a great opportunity.

See where your concerns are. See if your concern is with something from the past or with being used by the truth.

These are serious questions. They are not casual. Ask yourself what it is you *really* want, so that when this lifetime is finished, it is cleanly finished, completely finished, freely finished.

• • •

Last night I had a really powerful dream in which I built a huge bonfire. I would drench one flame with water, and another would pop up until finally, I was totally exhausted. I woke up and I said, "Let it burn." I just totally surrendered to it, and everything has been so wonderfully different since then.

I want to do more for everyone. I pray to heal them.

The healing for everyone is your willingness to experience this fire, to not dampen it.

This fire is the answer to your prayers. Realize that and then there is a shift in prayer. Rather than a prayer of supplication, offer a prayer of thanksgiving, a prayer of gratitude, a prayer of service.

Do you mean a prayer of being?

Being is not separate from true prayer. Gratefulness, devotion, and love are not separate from true prayer. As the removal of the mental veil reveals harmony and love, prayer becomes a great song of thanksgiving, and the rest of your life can be lived in honoring that. Honor the fire. Honor the removal of the veil. If you go back again to the old prayer of pleading, you dishonor what has already been revealed.

Let your whole life be prayer. You cried out. You begged for help. Help appeared for you as fire. The spiritual fire burns suffering up. It is the fire of realization. It is the fire of awakening. Live in greatest thanksgiving for that which has been revealed. Otherwise, the mind starts its searching activity again.

Don't pick up the old patterns of mind. Your prayer was stronger than the dampening, and all burst into flame, the flame of realization. Honor this. Let It guide you.

• • •

I feel drawn to service like a moth to a flame, but there is fear too.

The fire calls. The fire disintegrates all notions of server and served. If you answer this call with full attention and no idea of what the call should give you, your life will be a reward. Somehow, mysteriously, your life will be of service.

Let the call have you. Let it have your fears, your ideas, your plans, all—let it have all.

The fire burns brightly, and it lights up the night.

• • •

Christ is sometimes seen with a burning heart. I was wondering if you could talk about that. What that is, and what to do with it?

No amount of talk about it will satisfy you.

Isn't knowledge the greatest purifier?

In this instance, knowledge is the obstacle. Something known, some concept, is the obstacle. Satisfaction comes from direct experience. You have to discover the burning heart within you. You have to peel off the protections of conceptual knowledge so that you can discover what is beyond knowledge. You must discover that in which both knowledge and purification burn.

I guess I'm looking for resolution.

If you are looking for resolution through conceptual knowledge, you are looking in the wrong place.

So just remain in the feeling of the burning heart?

Dive into the center of that feeling. Don't waste any more time on the concept. Then your life is the resolution you have been seeking. You won't be asking anyone about a burning heart. You will be broadcasting it yourself; in words or not, in knowledge or not.

Knowledge that is innocent of the past, knowledge that is realized, revealed, alive, is Truth.

I guess the human nature is to move away from pain.

Yes, always trying to find out how to fix rather than to be. How to fix is called knowledge. For a moment, give up fixing and burn. There is no resolution until you are consumed.

When you are willing to burn, when you are willing to be consumed, when you stop fighting the call of your burning heart, when you just surrender into that, you realize you *are* That—not conceptually, but in reality.

• • •

Yesterday was the last day I had with someone who means a lot to me, and I was experiencing a great deal of pain. I went to satsang and just trusted and accepted the encouragement you gave us to surrender absolutely. Everything I saw, I just looked for well-being, and peace was really there!

I hope to serve That.

You do. Your report serves that. The willingness to surrender and to ask, "Is this true?" is already service. Then you see for yourself. It is very good you have recognized that which you love to be everywhere. Now recognize that truth is given freely and completely, and the more you give it, the more you discover it. It cannot be hoarded. It cannot be saved. If you give it to everything you see in every moment, you discover something unspeakable.

Self-Doubt: The Last Obstacle

Self-doubt and Self-distrust are impostors of true questioning. They have been used for socialization throughout time. True questioning of preconceived assumptions, your own and those of your culture's, of the past, of religions, of governments, and of politics of all kinds is an act of reflective intelligence.

To doubt the perfection of your personality, or the power of your body, or the wisdom of your thinking process is legitimate and even wise. To doubt who you are, to doubt the truth of Truth, is a waste of time at best. A waste of time that is a proven formula for suffering.

Ramana said that Self-doubt is the last obstacle. It is the final play of the mind. The mind is a great and wondrous power. It is the power to say no, the power to doubt, the power to deny. Now I am asking you to put that power aside, to not know, to not doubt, to be still.

Self-doubt is based on belief in your image of yourself as reality. With that image is attached an idea that right and wrong look a certain way. Living bound to this image and evaluation of self is called conditioned existence. The fear of releasing ideas of yourself is based on the fear that without those ideas, you will certainly do it wrong. You believe that at your core, you really *are* wrong. This belief is an indication of original sin, the original mistake.

Right and wrong as moral codes have an important place. Images of right and wrong have an important place. But finally, when you are called to know the truth of who you are, you cannot look to any image. You cannot look to anyone else's evaluation. If you have some picture of what enlightenment or freedom or right or wrong looks like, then you are duped by conditioned existence. All of these images are present in your mind only as you refer to the historical past. Horrible, wrong events occurred in the past, as did wondrous, right events. There is much to learn from history. History is a long, continuing story of the build up of the arrogance of mind, the horror that is the result of that arrogance, the release from that arrogance, and the humbling and peace that follow. End your long story with the humbling of the mind before truth.

Doubt the power of the mind, but do not doubt your Self. Do not give your mind such absolute power. The mind does not know how to make good use of such power. It just spins with it. The mind with illusions of absolute power is a tyrant. We can certainly see that throughout history, without a doubt! The mind is a beautiful servant. All of the intellect and all of your life experiences can be, and potentially are, in service to truth, in service to true Self. But first, doubt must be obliterated.

If you doubt your Self, the truth of your Self, you will suffer and search for release from this suffering through thought, emotion, and physical circumstance.

Do you understand this? I am not saying don't doubt your circumstances. I am saying don't doubt your Self. Your Self is bigger than any circumstance. Your Self is bigger than any thought, be it of grandiosity or worthlessness. It is before any emotion, after any emotion, and finally, as you will see, during every thought, emotion, and circumstance.

What a release when the old structures of mind fall. All the conditioning is like scaffolding, but scaffolding is not made to be left standing. When the individual consciousness is at a certain point, the scaffolding naturally needs to come down. Tear the scaffolding down. It is time, or you would not be attracted to satsang. If you are not attracted to satsang, it is perhaps not time. That is fine. Keep your scaffolding. When you are on fire, when there is true desire to awaken, everything that has come before must be torn down.

You may like or dislike whatever image you have of yourself, whatever body you have, whatever personality you have, whatever accomplishments you have, but to discover the truth of who you are is to discover Self-love. Self-love is not anything that has to be maintained. It is inherent in Self-discovery. Self-love can never be taken away. Self-love is Self-knowledge, Self-discovery, Self-realization. Not who you think you are, but who you truly are. True Self is not discovered in any thought. Thoughts may arise, *I am woman, I am man, I am human, I am wonderful, I am horrible,* but these thoughts have nothing to do with Self. When you discover your Self, you will find no gender, no species, no qualification.

This is the truth: At the core, you are pure goodness. You are inconceivably lucky to discover this core of goodness. This discovery is your homecoming.

You are welcome home. Receive the nectar of home. It is the nectar of Self-recognition. Drink it. Allow it to be received in your being, and the disease of Self-doubt is cured. If you turn from it, if you put it on a shelf, if you make plans to drink it some other day, then you are liable to imagine you have lost it.

Drink the nectar of Self now. Just check inside and you will see that it is being offered. Check in the core of your being, and receive the mystery being offered there. Drink! When you have drunk your fill, you will overflow with nectar. You will offer it to any who come. This is holy communion. You and Truth are one. You are That!

The Gangaji Foundation

The Gangaji Foundation serves the truth of universal consciousness and the potential for individual and collective
recognition of peace, inherent in the core of all being. It is the
purpose of the Gangaji Foundation to forthrightly and
respectfully present the teaching and transmission of Gangaji
through the grace of Sri Ramana Maharshi and Sri H.W.L.
Poonjaji.

A non-profit organization, The Gangaji Foundation serves to
make Satsang with Gangaji available through programs,
retreats, books, and tapes. The Foundation also offers books
and tapes by and about Ramana Maharshi and Poonjaji. For
a complete schedule and catalog, please contact:

THE GANGAJI FOUNDATION
800-267-9205
e-mail: info@gangaji.org

Visit our web site at www.gangaji.org

Books and tapes by Poonjaji are also available from:
THE AVADUTA FOUNDATION
2888 Bluff Street, Suite 390
Boulder, CO 80301